E ACADEMIC XCELLENCE

*The role of
research in the
physical sciences
at undergraduate
institutions*

MICHAEL P. DOYLE, EDITOR

PUBLISHED BY RESEARCH CORPORATION
a foundation for the advancement of science

Design and production
Carmen Vitello, Editor
Research Corporation

All material not otherwise credited written by
Michael P. Doyle and Carmen Vitello.

Photos courtesy of the authors and their institutions.

Research Corporation
101 North Wilmot Road, Suite 250
Tucson, Arizona 85711

Copyright 2000 by Research Corporation

ISBN 0-9633504-5-5

Contents

IN PURSUIT OF EXCELLENCE

Let those teach others, who themselves excel;
And censure freely, who have written well.

—ALEXANDER POPE

From Samuel Johnson's *Dictionary of the English Language*, 1773:
Excellence: to have good qualities in a great degree; to be eminent; to be great.

Academics are a disparate group of individuals, bound together by a common suspicion about the motives of the college administration and a missionary zeal to share the wonders of their disciplines with all who venture their way. A common objective, certainly in the early stages of a career, is to be the best, and to be associated with a department, a college, a university that shares this vision. Indeed, it would be a strange individual who aspires to be second rate, to devote a life and career to being an inconspicuous part of a group of also-rans.

Yet excellence, though easy to define, is a difficult state to achieve and, once there, it is the most unstable state of a dynamic equilibrium. The essays that follow are personal reflections on the pursuit of excellence, written by individuals from highly diversified backgrounds who have labored in different settings and have followed distinctive paths toward a common objective.

If you take the time to examine institutions that have achieved a significant measure of distinction, a common thread emerges. Almost universally, *positive changes occurred as a result of the conviction and determination of a single individual.* The pursuit of excellence requires a champion who will demonstrate through personal example and commitment how important goals can be articulated, how the necessary resources can be assembled, and how true scholarship enhances the educational experiences of students and faculty alike. We hope that the sharing of these experiences may be useful to those of you with similar goals.

JOHN P. SCHAEFER, PRESIDENT
RESEARCH CORPORATION

Tucson, Arizona
December 1, 2000

SECTION I
ACHIEVING EXCELLENCE

I HEAR AND I FORGET

I SEE AND I REMEMBER

I DO AND I UNDERSTAND

—CHINESE PROVERB

NUMEROUS STUDIES HAVE SHOWN that the undergraduate programs most successful at producing scientists are those that include research and publication in refereed journals. That is, research activity helps the faculty keep current but it also leads to more positive results for the students. Often the defenders of research by the faculty are accused of not being concerned about students. The studies demonstrate, to the contrary, that students benefit from a research-based teaching environment. Students who have the opportunity for research complete their science programs in greater numbers than those who do not. That implies to me that what is good for the faculty is also good for the students.

Robert Gavin is President of the Cranbrook Educational Community, and a past president of Macalester College.

Robert Gavin

1 THE ROLE OF RESEARCH AT UNDERGRADUATE INSTITUTIONS: WHY IS IT NECESSARY TO DEFEND IT?

The pendulum seems to swing to and fro on the role of research for faculty at colleges and universities, especially those faculty who have responsibility for teaching undergraduates. Critics say that research takes the faculty away from teaching students, does nothing to help the student and is not good pedagogy. Supporters of research, on the other hand, argue that research activity plays a central role in keeping the faculty up to date in the field and improves their teaching.

Research: a philosophical and pedagogical necessity

I am firmly on the side of the necessity of faculty being engaged in research if they are to be good teachers, but it seems to me that many of these discussions do not emphasize enough two critical points. First, that there is a philosophical difference between the natural sciences and the humanities regarding how one determines the truth of statements or models. This philosophical difference concerns data, experiments and research and leads to conclusions about how the discipline should be taught. Second, most of the discussions concentrate on what is good for the faculty members and do not mention what has been demonstrated by numerous studies on what works for the students.

First, the philosophical point. The shift from authority to observation and experiment for deciding the correctness of an explanation is a fundamental contribution that the natural sciences have brought to intellectual inquiry. I do not want to get into the debate about the limits of the scientific approach or whether scientific investigations are sufficient or even better explanations. The explanations, because of the method, must be tentative, not absolute, and based on evidence, not authority. However, the most important point is that if one is to be educated about science and the scientific approach, faculty must use observation, experimental design, testing and interpretation of results integral to science teaching.

Second, many studies have shown that the undergraduate programs most successful at producing scientists are those that include research and publication in refereed journals. That is, research activity helps the faculty keep current but it also leads to more positive results for the students. Often the defenders of research by the faculty are accused of not being concerned about students. The studies demonstrate, to the contrary, that the students benefit from a research-based teaching environment. Students who have the opportunity for research complete their science programs in greater numbers than those who do not. That implies to me that what is good for the faculty is also good for the students.

Students who have the opportunity for research complete science programs in greater numbers than those who do not.

Research-based teaching

Good science courses, whether for science or non-science majors, teach about observation, experiment design and interpretation of data. That is, the courses include coverage of the methods of science, not only current scientific paradigms. Whether the student is to major in the natural sciences or elsewhere, the student should learn about the scientific method and not just be told the results of others. Courses that only present the current paradigm about how the universe works may be entertaining and interesting for the audience but do not teach the essence of the natural science disciplines.

This is not to suggest that students should be taught only by doing cutting-edge research. Prior to the undergraduate years, students should be involved in "hands-on" and "discovery" learning where they can develop their observational skills and learn for themselves that the correctness of an explanation can be determined by a well-designed experiment. Introducing young persons to science in this fashion not only prepares them well for research-based learning later but makes science much more engaging and fun.

Good introductory courses at the undergraduate level provide a bridge from "discovery" to actual research in the disciplines. However, simply having a laboratory associated with courses is not enough. Too often the laboratory portion of the course is a "fill-in-the-blanks" exercise rather than an opportunity to present students with a problem and having them discover the answer or design experiments to get at the answer.

Anyone who has taught research-based courses knows that it takes much more time and effort to teach in this fashion rather than only lecture. It is much easier to just "tell them the answer" than to ask them to design experiments which can lead to a better understanding of natu-

Defending Research in the 1920s

The question of the value of research in undergraduate education has been with us for a long time. In the first issue of the *Journal of Chemical Education* in 1924, Professor W.A. Patrick of Johns Hopkins University discussed the relationship of research to teaching. He stated that there is not a great need for research involvements by teachers since they interfere with the principal goals of education. His supporting rationale is interesting: "It is my belief that the task of laying the accumulated knowledge of chemistry before students is of sufficient magnitude to demand the entire strength and ability of any man. If we seek to improve the standard of chemical instruction by requiring the instructor to add to our store of knowledge by original investigation, as well as present students the known facts with clearness and enthusiasm, then I fear that either poor teaching or poor investigation will result."[1]

Now, of course, Patrick's remarks provoked the ire of a number of individuals, not the least of whom was Professor Harry Holmes of Oberlin College. Holmes had a distinguished career, serving as president of the American Chemical Society and a member of the National Research Council. In response to the article by Professor Patrick, he said, "I fear that this is a dangerous doctrine. Had Morley heeded such advice during his professorship at Adelbert College of Western Reserve University he would not have given science his great classic on the combining weights of oxygen and hydrogen." Holmes pointed out other examples of those who disagreed with Patrick's view that combining research and teaching would reduce the quality of both. He noted that his own consideration of research as important to good teaching had a great number of proponents, including the members of the National Research Council, not the least of which was Professor Albert Noyes. One of Holmes' comments draws attention to some key values of research in undergraduate education. He said, "A stimulating freshness and a feeling of authority come to the college teacher as he unravels the secrets of science. The teacher profits, the great body of science profits, and the pupil profits. The pupil feels that he's near one of the fresh springs that feed the stream of knowledge into which he has been dipping." Holmes continued, "It is essential that the teacher do research work. He should comb the subject of chemistry from end to end for facts and methods of exposition that will make such facts alive and real to his students."[2]

ral phenomena. Teaching students to think for themselves requires creativity from the teacher and opportunities for students to experiment with ideas.

In science, to be student-centered in your teaching is to teach them the essence of your discipline: experiential design, observation and hypothesis-testing through experiment. That is the strength of research-based teaching and the reason for having research-active faculty who are prepared to teach in that fashion.

What is the role of lectures?

Promotion of research-based teaching is not meant to imply that lectures should play no role in science education. Well-organized lectures play an important role in teaching but they should not be relied upon as a substitute for research experience. The lecture should provide the background on what has been learned over the years through observation and experimentation. Learning about the experiments which were critical to the establishment of the laws of thermodynamics or the double helix structure of DNA or the Big Bang model helps the student see the power of a well-designed experiment. Lectures are important but they are not the place where students develop their observational and data-gathering skills or their ability to design experiments.

What is the role of textbooks?

Much is made of the importance of textbooks. In my opinion, textbooks provide a supplement to the lectures and provide the student with examples of experiments that support current theories about the properties of the universe.

In other words, textbooks, like lectures are important supplemental aids to science instruction. There is no need to reinvent the wheel with each generation. Textbooks allow us to learn our scientific history and catalog the facts. However, one should not place the learning of facts, an important exercise, on the same level of importance as the necessity to learn about observation, experimental design and repeatability in science.

What is the role of publishing?

The recent study by Baughman and Goldman, "College Rankings and Faculty Publications: Are They Related?"[3] demonstrates that college rank and rate of publication by the faculty are closely related (table, right). Those colleges with the highest rates of faculty publication hold the best academic reputations. This should surprise no one. These colleges are considered good by just about any ranking system because the faculty at these institutions are shaping the arguments in their disciplines, are engaged with their peers in intellectual dialog and they allow their students to be fully engaged in this process through research-based teaching.

If research-based education is consistently ranked as the best way to educate scientists, why not come to the conclusion that research should be expected?

Two books published by Ernest L. Boyer, *College: The Undergraduate Experience in America*[4] and *Scholarship Reconsidered: Priorities of the Professoriate*,[5] have been cited by many to justify not doing research and publication at undergraduate institutions. The books do, in this author's opinion, create an unfortunate dichotomy between teaching and research but do not present a convincing case against publishing as an important activity for faculty, or support the position that it would be much better to have faculty concentrate on pedagogy than research to improve their teaching (see insert, page 21).

Scholarship Reconsidered reports responses to a national survey of faculty opinion regarding publishing, research and tenure.[6] The survey results show that research and publication are thought to play a large role

Median Number of ISI[a] Entries per 100 Faculty Members by Barron's Ranking and Carnegie Classifications (Undergraduate Listing Only[b])[7]

Carnegie Classification	Median Number of ISI Entries per 100 Faculty Members					
	Barron's Ranking[c] (lowest → highest)					
	1	2	3	4	5	6
Master's I	3.3	6.2	7.0	17.0	20.2	*
	(35)	(92)	(235)	(42)	(7)	(0)
Master's II	0.9	2.2	3.1	6.3	*	*
	(12)	(15)	(54)	(8)	(1)	(0)
Baccalaureate I	*	8.9	10.1	14.9	31.4	45.7
	(0)	(3)	(44)	(62)	(41)	(14)
Baccalaureate II	0	1.7	2.2	2.7	*	*
	(60)	(122)	(213)	(29)	(1)	(0)

[a] Institute for Scientific Information
[b] The same relationships exist in research and doctoral institutions.
[c] Figure in parentheses represents the number of institutions in each group.
* indicates fewer than three institutions fall into this group.

in faculty tenure decisions and that many faculty would prefer that it not be so. However, both books call for scholarship, which implies to me that both research and publication in refereed journals are essential activities of the profession. Boyer stated in *College* "Scholarship is not an esoteric appendage; it is at the heart of what the profession is all about . . ." and "to weaken faculty commitment for scholarship . . . is to undermine the undergraduate experience, regardless of the academic setting." [8] And in *Scholarship Reconsidered* Boyer calls for scholarship and its application to problems of society ". . . to sustain the vitality of higher education in our time, a new vision of scholarship is required, one dedicated not only to the renewal of the academy but, ultimately, to the renewal of society itself." [9]

If research-based education is consistently ranked as the best way to educate scientists and it leads to higher completion rates, why not come to the conclusion that research, and the evaluation of that research through publication, should be expected? The concern should be about what can be done post-tenure to ensure that faculty are not neglecting research and publication. Publishing research articles, especially those done in collaboration with undergraduate students, should be expected, encouraged and supported both before and after the tenure decision.

What is required to have successful programs?

There are three critical elements that must work in concert: faculty committed to research-based pedagogy, an administration that recognizes and supports the research-based approach, and resources to support the laboratories, equipment and supplies needed for research. As with so many other things, two out of three is not sufficient.

Committed faculty and administrators must have the resources. The resources and a committed administration cannot succeed with a recalcitrant faculty. And, committed faculty who get the resources can be frustrated by an unsympathetic administration.

Who are the key partners for successful science programs?

The most successful programs have both a bottom-up and a top-down support system. The president, provost, deans and department chairs work with faculty to ensure that resources are obtained from the college or university funds as well as from corporations, foundations and government agencies.

Administrations cannot force a research-based approach on faculty who do not have a passion for research and, on the other hand, energetic faculty can be worn down by an administration which is unwilling to work with them to make the research-based curriculum a reality.

Undergraduate science education received a very positive boost from a collaborative approach involving presidents, deans and faculty through the formation of the so-called Oberlin Group in 1985 and 1986. Prior to the gatherings, a study was made to determine which colleges that had been most successful in producing graduates who went on to complete Ph.D. degrees in the natural sciences. In line with several other studies, the data showed that the stronger the research of faculty at the college the greater the percentage of graduates who went on to complete Ph.D.'s. This study was used as a discussion document for the presidents of forty-eight of those colleges at a conference held at Oberlin College (page 16).

As a direct result of these meetings there were many new programs initiated to support undergraduate research. Major foundations such as the Pew Charitable Trust, the Howard Hughes Medical Institute and the NSF, opened new programs to support the natural sciences at undergraduate institutions. The activities of the Council on Undergraduate Research (CUR; page 97) were expanded at about the same time to include new disciplines and faculty at colleges other than the group that gathered at Oberlin. All in all, the meetings stimulated an increase in research at the undergraduate level.

It has been fifteen years since the Oberlin meetings. Today, few of the fifty presidents who attended those conferences are still in office. Research Corporation, which played such a key role in the resurgence of research at these schools during the decade from 1985 through 1995, is now working with the Camille and Henry Dreyfus Foundation, the W. M. Keck Foundation, the M. J. Murdock Charitable Trust, and the Robert A. Welch Foundation to provide a service to undergraduate science by sponsoring another "Oberlin 50" type meeting to discuss the current state of research support and the needs of today (see page 199).

What works?

We have known for a long time what works in the education of scientists: research-based education. However, the case needs to be made anew nearly every decade. The support for research is waning and now is the time voices need to be raised to ensure that we do not back away from the engine that has been driving our economy and helping us to understand the universe in which we live. Æ

THE OBERLIN CONFERENCE

"The Future of Science at Liberal Arts Colleges" conference, subsequently known as the "Oberlin Conference," was held in Oberlin, Ohio, June 9–10, 1985. Organized by S. Frederick Starr, then president of Oberlin College, the conference set out to enable presidents of nearly fifty colleges of arts and sciences to assess the state of teaching and research in science at their institutions. The conference also sought to bring an appreciation of the significance of such work to higher education as a whole and to the nation, to estimate the resources necessary to preserve and enhance this national asset, and to suggest means of attracting such resources.

The conclusions that could be drawn from the associated study were summarized in a report by President Starr:[10]

> Broadly speaking, the data show that leading liberal arts colleges rank at or near the top of all American institutions of higher education—including multiversities and major centers of research—in the training of scientists. They show that this success is due significantly to the close link between teaching and faculty research that exists on such campuses. They show that the premier colleges have been nearly immune to the erosion of student interest in science that has recently afflicted major research universities and the nation. Finally they show that this record of accomplishment has been financed mainly by the institutions themselves and by tuition payments, the level of federal support going to science programs in liberal arts colleges having diminished even as support for university centers has grown. In other words, this report indicates that leading liberal arts colleges are not only exceptionally productive in the natural sciences, but also relatively cost-effective.

The conference report identified what were found to be the essential aspects of quality education in the sciences. The foremost component of the successful education of scientists was judged to be the science faculty. In the forty-eight participating institutions, one-quarter of the teaching staff was devoted to the natural sciences. About half were tenured and one-quarter held tenure-track positions. "The value of my undergraduate program was the individual attention . . . ," an astronomer at one of the participating institutions wrote. "Every class was given by a Ph.D. 'teacher-scholar,' never by a graduate student."[11]

Research and scholarly activity were "the next essential ingredients" to be considered in maintaining excellence so that faculty could be at the "cutting edge of their disciplines." To be able to teach the skills essential to scientific inquiry, "faculty members themselves must be professionally active in their fields." A definition of "cutting edge" was not given.

Among the data made available with this study was the surprising fact that 60 percent of the science faculty from the forty-eight participating institutions published journal articles in the five-year span from 1979–1980 through 1983–84, and the average publication rate for all science faculty was 0.56 per faculty member per year. Furthermore, these faculty published more than one literature review every four years, and a total of 351 books. It was also reported that in 1983–84 there were 45.5 paid student assistants doing undergraduate research per institution surveyed. The validity of these numbers was not questioned.

However, "the primary hallmark of undergraduate science education" at the participating liberal arts institutions was the faculty-student interaction which afforded the opportunity for students to do research alongside a "distinguished" faculty member.

> The development of true command of scientific disciplines requires substantial hands-on experience in the laboratory; . . . careful training in research methodology; and the interactive give and take with professors and peers. . . . These liberal arts colleges and their . . . science faculties create an unsurpassed environment for providing science students abundant, close interaction with mentors, extensive research experience at the undergraduate level, and the opportunity to publish research findings.

The Oberlin report's last essential element for producing quality science education was the financial investment in the future of American science with monies to fund research, support faculty, and provide assistance for students. The next year's conference report ("Maintaining America's Scientific Productivity"[12]) reached the conclusion that the top liberal arts colleges would have to invest a total of one billion dollars within ten years if they were to maintain their unique position in basic science education and research. There has not been a subsequent report from this group of institutions.

NﾠATIONAL RECOGNITION IS OBTAINED by growing a reputation that can be identified beyond your local confines. You may be the institution's best teacher, and students love to hear every word that you utter, but if you don't stand out relative to faculty in other institutions you have only local influence. You may have administrative skills comparable to those of corporate managers, but if these skills are applied only in local committees you have only local influence. You may perform experiments with students that stimulate in them intense interest in science, but unless those experiments lead to a definable outcome, your influence will only be transient.

Michael P. Doyle is Vice President of Research Corporation.

Michael P. Doyle

2 ACHIEVING A NATIONAL REPUTATION FOR EXCELLENCE

How many professions expect their members to perform the same work when hired as when approaching retirement? At many academic institutions, all faculty are considered to be equal, have the same teaching loads, office and laboratory space, and allocations for services and supplies; they are differentiated by years of service which is often the primary determinant of their salary. In small departments, a faculty member often teaches the same courses year after year, so that one must ask: How many times does a faculty member teach the same course before its content fails to change? I recall one instructor who taught with transparencies, timing correctly the minutes required by students to transcribe the transparency text and figures into their notebooks, but did not utter a word of lecture.

How many times does a faculty member teach the same course before its content fails to change?

Few professional careers offer the stability of tenure—that academic perogative which frees a faculty member from considerations of unemployment. In colleges and universities a faculty member is given six years to validate the optimism of colleagues during the initial interview. Within these six short years that faculty member must meet the expectations of academic administrators and colleagues, which are sometimes in conflict, not offend anyone who has influence on the decision, and so enamor students as to draw from them their firm support.

With tenure comes promotion—from assistant to associate professor—and, if appropriate standards are met, eventually to full professor. These then are the stepping stones for the faculty member: tenure and promotion. What remains constant, like death and taxes, is Chemistry 121. Teaching that course and supervising its laboratory are the established foci of this career from beginning to end.

Change is good

Few look forward to change. We fondly look back on the post-Sputnik years as a Golden Age for science, with streams of money flowing into academic institutions to support the physical sciences, but few undergraduate institutions took advantage of this opportunity. It's easier to

The Beginnings of Undergraduate Research

Undergraduate research has been the most exciting educational development of the second half of the twentieth century. In the pre-World War II era, students were involved in many laboratories and were watching the conduct of experiments and learning about the process of discovery. This was especially true in undergraduate institutions where junior and senior students were the principal workforce. In universities with graduate programs there was less need to involve undergraduate students; graduate students were available and had as their principal objective the conduct of research.

Just following the end of World War II, Research Corporation designed a funding initiative, the Frederick Gardner Cottrell program, to provide incentive for scientists to return to colleges and universities, rather than joining the industrial and federal research laboratories into which they had been "drafted" for the course of the war. These grants made possible full-time summer research for selected undergraduate students.[1]

Faculty members who were performing research during the summer needed assistants and, without the cadre of free labor available when classes were in session, found that student employment provided the necessary workforce. No longer limited by the time constraints of course work, students became more intimately involved in actual experimentation. By the end of the summer, they were well-versed in experimental details and filled with the excitement of potential new discoveries.

With the advent of the new academic year, faculty curtailed their research in order to prepare for classes, but their students, enthusiastic with experience from their summer research engagements, came into the laboratory with regularity to continue their experimentation. Out of this was born the beginnings of undergraduate research in the sciences.

continue doing the same thing than to potentially attract criticism, or even a lawsuit, because of change. Is that why the performance of fundamental research, with its unknown consequences, is treated with skepticism at so many colleges and universities?

The fact is that few faculty respond to more than personal or immediate directives or incentives. If you personally have the will or drive to be a star, you will direct your life towards that end. Otherwise, the president of the college or the dean of the division sets the directive; you are less likely to respond to an organization more distant than that immediate influence. There is less likelihood today than when I started in 1968, that faculty will organize a meeting—as did happen, however unjustly, several times at Hope College—to plan to "dump the president." A vote of "no confidence" in an administrator is sufficiently rare that one can expect to hear of every instance in the *Chronicle of Higher Education*.

With the endowments of some private undergraduate institutions now at or above $1 billion, will these institutions take more or fewer risks? Will they exert more or less control over faculty professional activities? Will scholarship be encouraged or discouraged? The president of a financially well-endowed university once told me that the overall quality of his school depended, in large measure, on parallel excellence in all departments, so it was best to hold back fast moving departments so that the others could catch up.

Deny tenure because the faculty member did not meet expectations in research— "why, that's immoral," shouted a faculty member from a church-affiliated undergraduate institution. "A faculty member is hired to teach, not to do research. Research distracts a faculty member from his or her primary responsibility [see insert below]." How long before this faculty member teaches students that the concepts in general chemistry are irrefutable and change is impractical? Isn't it easier to teach the introductory course when you don't have anything new to say?

A parent once wrote to me, "You are not making chemistry fun for my son. I sent him to your institution so that he could enjoy his courses and not be overwhelmed by course content appropriate only for students who plan to enter graduate school." To which I replied, "I have the responsibility to bring the students in my charge to their potential, whether their career aspiration is medicine, or law, or politics. I do not believe that a primary goal of a college course should be to make its content 'fun' for its participants." Yet, today, a primary concern of new faculty, especially those at private undergraduate institutions, is the impact that stu-

---

But at the undergraduate level . . . research work often competes with classroom obligations, both in time and content. Faculty assigned to teach such courses frequently must take short cuts in their research or rely heavily on teaching assistants. . . . We find it revealing, for example, that in our surveys more than half of the faculty at research and doctorate institutions agreed that at their institution "the pressure to publish reduces the quality of teaching."

—Scholarship Reconsidered, Ernest L. Boyer, 1990[2]

---

dent evaluations have on their promotion and tenure. Are they only expected to make their course "fun" for students? What measure is used for teaching effectiveness by faculty?

A primary concern of new faculty is the impact that student evaluations have on their promotion and tenure.

Doesn't a college or university have the responsibility to create opportunities for its students beyond what might have been possible in the absence of that institution? For a select few institutions these opportunities may be the association with other students, sons and daughters of the leaders of society. For most institutions, however, increasing emphasis will have to be placed on realized benefit to compensate for cost-benefit considerations by parents. And unlike the past, benefit will be measured in career opportunities, not in the breadth of student experiences.

Who opens the doors to careers?

The faculty whose reputations extend beyond the local campus open doors to their students' careers. Do the names Corwin Hansch (Pomona College) or Harold Heine (Bucknell University) ring a bell? What about National Academy of Sciences member Jerry Gollub (Haverford College)? Hansch and Heine were the first two recipients of the American Chemical Society Award for Research at Undergraduate Institutions sponsored by Research Corporation, and Corwin was also the 1999 recipient of the ACS Award in Medicinal Chemistry. Gollub, a physicist, was elected to the National Academy in 1993, not because of his association with Haverford but because of the opportunities afforded to him, in part, by Haverford.

These faculty, and others like them, open doors for their students that would otherwise have been closed. At a college that is local in its influence, a faculty member may be able to call an acquaintance in the local area to seek a position for his or her student. A faculty member

A faculty member who has regional recognition can assist students regionally, but one who has a national reputation opens doors virtually everywhere.

who has regional recognition can assist students regionally, but one who has a national reputation opens doors virtually everywhere. If I were a parent looking for opportunities for my children, I would certainly ask about the national standing of the faculty. By what measure are they known nationally? How can their reputations assist my son or daughter?

I have never received a local award that recognized either my teach-

---

FACULTY INTEREST = STUDENT PRODUCTIVITY

The Wooster Conference on teaching and research (sponsored by the American Chemical Society and supported by the National Science Foundation) in 1959 divided liberal arts colleges into four categories—very productive, productive, borderline, and unproductive—on the basis of the number of chemistry graduates that had earned the Ph.D. in chemistry. . . . All of the participants in the conference agreed that personal contacts between students and faculty stimulate interest in chemistry and a desire to pursue graduate work.[3]

---

ing or my research. Those, especially the former, were generally given because of popularity, longevity, or factors peculiar to the local selection committee, but rarely having to do with long-term impact. I recall those instances when faculty who had been denied tenure were accorded college-teaching honors because those electing the individuals wished to protest the tenure decision. I have generally found that research universities do a better job recognizing their faculty for teaching effectiveness and impact than do undergraduate institutions.

How does one acquire a national reputation?

Is reputation based on the institution itself, or is it solely determined by the efforts of the faculty member? Of course, neither is generally applicable. Even the "best" undergraduate institutions have weak departments and inactive faculty. And it is the exception, rather than the rule, that a faculty member from an undistinguished institution will achieve national standing in his or her profession.

National recognition is obtained by growing a reputation that can be identified beyond your local confines. You may be the institution's best teacher, and students love to hear every word that you utter, but if you don't stand out relative to faculty in other institutions you only have local influence. You may have administrative skills comparable to those of corporate managers, but if these skills are only applied in local committees you only have local influence. You may perform experiments with students that stimulate in them intense interest in science, but unless those experiments lead to a definable outcome, your influence will only be transient.

There are many ways to achieve national recognition but, contrary to popular belief, there are precious few channels through which individual

23

excellence is recognized, and only one provides an abundance of opportunities for individual achievements. In science, individual achievements are recognized through publications in peer-reviewed journals and from grants and awards provided by funding agencies and foundations. Here discovery, the ability to complete a project, and advancements in science and education are rewarded. Those making the judgment are respected members of the national or international community, and their views are generally given as experts in the area of science or science education without prejudice. If accepted, the work submitted reaches a visibility that extends the outreach of the individual beyond the local college environment. Publication and grants or awards go hand-in-hand. The quality of the publications can be equated with the level of funding or the extent of awards, either in scientific research or education.

In science individual achievements are recognized through publications in peer-reviewed journals and from grants and awards.

Peer review

"Peer review" is the key to understanding quality. Articles submitted to the *Proceedings of the Local Academy of Arts and Sciences* rarely pass through peer review, and there are some professional journals that accept virtually everything submitted to them. No one knowledgeable in a profession is fooled by numbers (see insert, page 25). Publication in these journals actually detracts from the reputation of the faculty member.

Also, contrary to popular belief, presentations made by students in student symposia at professional meetings are not major outlets for scientific discovery but are for the educational benefit of the students. They are not like publications, and those that attend do so for reasons other than science advancement. Faculty presentations are generally also of educational benefit for them, allowing their work to be seen by an audience that they do not ordinarily reach. Presentations, even when they require an abstract, are not peer reviewed. I do not wish to imply that presentations by either students or faculty should not be made, for they do have significant benefits, but they are not the activity that brings national recognition to either the faculty member or the institution.

I have watched how some colleges and universities award "research grants" to their faculty from a pool of funds designated to stimulate "research." A faculty member submits a proposal to a committee for what the institution calls "peer review." However, that committee almost al-

THE IMPACT FACTOR

Samuel C. Bradford, a former librarian of the Science Museum in London, observed that there are diminishing returns in trying to cover the literature exhaustively. Stated as *Bradford's Law,* his observation can be interpreted as "a small percentage of journals account for a large percentage of what is published." The corollary, "an even smaller number of journals account for what is cited," is even more relevant in scientific publishing today.

Journal Citation Reports, published by the Institute for Scientific Information (ISI), provides a systematic means for determining the relative importance of science and social science journals within their subject categories (biochemistry and molecular biology, chemistry, medicine, and physics, for example). Journals that have the highest impact factor have the greatest potential for advancing a career. Why are the *Journal of the American Chemical Society* and *Physical Review Letters* considered to be premier journals? It is because their impact factor is so high.

Who is held in higher regard—the faculty member who publishes one paper per year in a high-impact journal or the one who publishes five papers per year in a low-impact journal? The answer is clear. High impact signifies greater importance to the science and a higher probability that other scientists will read the paper and be influenced by it. However, not all good science can or should be published only in the high-impact journals, and frequency of publication is important. Still, unless there is a sprinkling of high-impact journals in a faculty member's vitae, how can one judge the overall importance to science of that faculty member's research activities?

ways consists entirely of faculty from the same institution—a condition avoided in the external community because of the potential for prejudice, both in acceptance or denial, and because of the absence of experts who are able to review potential for technical achievement and impact. You may have heard the same complaints as I have from internal committee members: "I can't understand this!"; "It is written with too many technical terms!"; "Joan received an award two years ago—let someone else have a chance." Few institutions have specific goals for internal grants through which outcome could be monitored and evaluated. Proposals for sabbatical leaves are too often judged internally in the same way.

I recently visited an institution that had created an endowment for research. The internal awards, recommended by an internal committee and approved by the dean and president, were available for faculty summer salary and undergraduate student support. When asked "What would occur if one of the faculty-award recipients was notified of a comparably-sized research grant from an external foundation or agency?" the answer given was that the faculty member would have to return the internal award so that the funds could be reallocated to a faculty member who did not have external support. Internal programs are not necessarily intended to reward professional achievements, and they can be disincentives to writing proposals that seek external support.

You will note that up to now I have included both science and science education as appropriate to building national reputations. There are significant differences between them, however. If your reputation is to be built upon science careers for students and your own involvement in investigative scholarship, then research in the sciences is the appropriate pathway. If your reputation is to be built upon education, with teaching careers for students and innovations in curricular development a focus, the appropriate pathway is science education. However, make no mistake; both pathways to national reputations are measured in the same way—through publications and grants or awards. You should also realize that there is a difference between a NSF Research in Undergraduate Institutions (REU) grant and a NSF Research Experiences for Undergraduates (RUI) grant, and that a Course and Curriculum Laboratory Improvement (CCLI; Appendix, page 192) grant is really a department award and should not be listed by an individual faculty member as a measure of standing in either education or research.

Barriers to excellence

Science is often accused of being elitist and reluctant to open its doors to newcomers, but then so is science education. Perception of an inner closed circle depends on many factors, few of which are related to science. I recall one of several forays to the Division of Chemical Education of the American Chemical Society to discuss their willingness to serve as a home for an award for research at an undergraduate institution. Members of the executive committee asked, "What do we need with another award? We already have one!" Their concern was that the new award might diminish the one already in place with the title of "for Chemical Education." This consideration leads to another question—why is there only one American Chemical Society award for education when there is a vast array of awards for research and service?

At one Midwestern college I heard this description from a faculty member recently attracted to the institution: "I was told to forgo a post-doctoral experience because my department chair said that with a Ph.D. degree I knew how to do research. I should come directly to the college so that I could learn how to teach." Unfortunately, this misconception can be found at a large number of predominantly undergraduate institutions whose faculty in science are hired without expectations of post-doctoral experience. Yet the absence of postdoctoral experience reduces a faculty member's ability to synthesize his or her independent research program. At least at Research Corporation, this limits a proposal from being funded—not because of any internal restriction but because a faculty member without postdoctoral experience is rarely able to prepare a proposal that is not directly related only to his or her graduate experience. In other words, your perception of the world is limited if you haven't experienced many of its parts.

The Japanese system of higher education is significantly different from our own. In science, emphasis is placed on masters-level degrees rather than on the Ph.D. which is only meant for those seeking university positions or willing to undertake managerial positions in industry. The M.S. degree is sufficient for those who enter industry. One shouldn't spend too much time advancing through degrees when the institution can offer the experience that is more suitable. Does teaching the introductory course really require a Ph.D. degree? However, the advanced courses do require advanced knowledge and understanding, and those who would venture to advance scientific understanding need further extension in critical thinking and evaluation. Aren't undergraduate institutions that take faculty without postdoctoral experience limiting themselves and their faculty?

Achieving a national reputation for excellence means being distinctive—not ordinary—and encouraging professionalism.

Achieving a national reputation for excellence means being distinctive—not ordinary—and encouraging professionalism. Extraordinary institutions are not necessarily those that are the most financially well-endowed. Sometimes the achievements of one faculty member can enhance the reputation of an entire institution. A key element is to "never say no" to innovation, even when financial resources do not appear to be in hand. "We can do this together" is an apt response, and the outcome is generally highly beneficial. Æ

THE QUEST FOR NEW KNOWLEDGE and new solutions to problems is influencing how professors teach and students learn science. Students learn science today by doing it, and obviously doing science means doing research or engaging in research-like activities. Science instruction today focuses less and less on developing a student's ability to follow the instructions for a time-honored experiment or to replicate some already established results. While those activities remain valid and vital parts of scientific education, they can no longer be confused with the real thing. Today, we want to give students a chance to do the real thing because we know that it energizes them even as it provides an extremely effective vehicle for their learning.

Richard Warch is President of Lawrence University.

RICHARD WARCH

3 IF YOU BUILD IT, THEY WILL COME ... AND STAY

I MUST CONFESS THAT AT TIMES I resonate to the position once described by W. H. Auden: "When I find myself in the company of scientists," he wrote, "I feel like a shabby curate who has strayed by accident into a drawing room full of dukes." Fortunately, my science colleagues at Lawrence University rarely make me feel shabby, and even more rarely do they try to intimidate me by acting like royalty. Nonetheless, the worlds they inhabit and the work they pursue often appear quite rarefied, at least to this humanities-educated college president.

That being stipulated, as the lawyers say, I begin by claiming that I have gradually come to understand and appreciate how science faculty practice their trade. More to the point of this essay, I have come to value and enthusiastically promote what I view as a strong science program. The word "program" is pivotal here. At Lawrence, as at other science-active liberal arts colleges, education in the sciences is not and cannot be confined simply to a curriculum, cannot be conveyed merely through some array of courses offered by individual departments on an annual basis, however essential and excellent they may be. Instead, I have come to realize, good science instruction emerges from broad-gauge programs, usually, though not necessarily, departmental programs, offering a rich and diverse fare that significantly supplements and extends the curriculum. Ingredients of such an effort include ongoing research programs in which students can pursue undergraduate research, summer internships for undergraduate majors and non-majors, regular visits by prominent scientists, frequent scientific colloquia, professionally informed advising, and an array of other departmental or extra-departmental activities that foster community, pride, esprit, and shared values among students and faculty alike.

Good science instruction emerges from broad-gauge programs.

Programs of this sort have been developing for some time at Lawrence. What differentiates the present situation from the past are the increasingly diverse elements in such programs and the widespread commitment to research-based teaching. Strong endorsements of undergraduate research have come to permeate the teaching and learning of science, sometimes appearing even at the introductory level and certainly mani-

> *Introductory college [science] courses remain unapologetically competitive, selective and intimidating, designed to winnow out all but the "top tier," and . . . there is little attempt to create a sense of "community" among average students of science. Even good students are often given the wrong message that there is no room in science for people like themselves.*
>
> —They're Not Dumb, They're Different: Stalking the Second Tier, *Sheila Tobias, 1990* [1]

festing themselves in various ways at the advanced undergraduate level. In recent years, scientists and science educators—and even college presidents—have recognized that the tradition of science education in this country, once dominated by the sense that science existed for a select few, should be abandoned. Too often, introductory science courses acted as filters rather than pumps, eliminating those students whose "aptitude"

Too often, introductory science courses acted as filters rather than pumps.

for science seemed less robust in order to devote greater attention to students whose abilities met the high standards of the field and who could "do the work" (see insert

above). Fortunately, this mentality is on the wane, especially at liberal arts colleges like Lawrence.

What is the "work" of science?

The practitioners claim that the work of science entails the quest for new laws, new theories, and new understandings of new phenomena. Increasingly, this quest for new knowledge and new solutions to problems is influencing how professors teach and students learn science. Students learn science today by doing it, and obviously doing science means doing research or engaging in research-like activities. Research, someone has noted, has been called good business or a game, when in fact it is really a state of mind. Instilling that state in students' minds is driving contemporary science education. Science instruction today focuses less and less on developing a student's ability to follow the instructions for a time-honored experiment or to replicate some already established results. While those activities remain valid and vital parts of scientific education, they can no longer be confused with the real thing. Today, we want to give students a chance to do the real thing because we know that it energizes them even as it provides an extremely effective vehicle for learning.

Introductory pieties aside, developing good science programs that include the aforementioned ingredients and embrace considerable research emphasis is not merely a matter of uttering encouragement, although there is a time and place for that. At Lawrence, we have found that it requires considerable investment of time, talent, and resources. The case in point that I want to focus on here is physics. About a dozen years ago, the two senior members of the Lawrence physics department, John Brandenberger and David Cook, began to contemplate the future, an undertaking not without its pitfalls and hazards. They were then concerned with the drawing power of their department and, after much reflection, reached the judgment that physics simply could not continue as it was in the hope that the admissions office would turn up enough talented freshmen to populate its courses. In short, they understood Einstein's adage that insanity is "doing the same thing over and over again and expecting different results." Consequently, they decided that the moment had come to invest time, energy and resources into the development of "signature" activities (that was my term at the time, a term that still is in the process of being defined at Lawrence) within the department that would be distinctive, would be attractive to students, and would energize the faculty. Building on their own research expertise and interests, they selected laser physics and computational physics as the initial foci, areas which in those days were underrepresented, if not unrepresented, in undergraduate physics departments nationwide. And then the fun began.

They decided that the moment had come to invest time, energy and resources into the development of "signature" activities.

The "Laser Palace"

Our first undertaking was to steal a line and an idea from the movie, *Field of Dreams* and take the leap of faith that if we built it, they would come. The "it" in that sentence referred in the first instance to a laser facility, which we dubbed the "Laser Palace," a term chosen in part as a jocular reflection on the fact that what Professor Brandenberger had in mind was going to require significant investments to acquire new equipment and to reconfigure appropriate space. My task, as the college president, was to encourage this undertaking and help Brandenberger and Cook secure the necessary resources (which would, for these two projects, eventually reach about $500,000). As it turned out, the case we were able to articulate proved persuasive to a number of funding agencies.

Working in the Laser Palace, Dr. Brandenberger and students examine the spectral lineshape of an open-frame, narrow-bore, helium-neon laser.

Indeed, with grants in hand, we created a laser facility consisting of several labs, the largest of which was formally named "Laser Palace" with the moniker displayed in bright neon lights (above). A year or so later, we replicated the feat for Professor Cook's initiative in computational physics by creating a lab of high-end workstations that enabled a second signature program in physics to take off as well.

Take off it did, but not without some other ingredients. Probably the most important of these was the creation of physics recruitment weekends for prospective students. Begun in 1987 for laser physics—computational physics was added a year or two later—this endeavor still brings forty invitees to campus annually for a weekend of hands-on experiments and experiences in laser and computational physics along with the recently-added areas of X-ray diffraction and plasma physics. During these weekends, prospective students work closely with faculty members and Lawrence undergraduates on a range of experiments and find them both exciting and promising. Roughly 30 percent of the students who attend these events matriculate at Lawrence. So, having built it, they do come. Four years after we launched these physics workshops, the number of graduating majors increased from roughly five per year to more than ten per year, and the numbers of students graduating with honors and electing to go on to graduate or professional school increased comparably. In the past decade, over 50 percent of the physics graduates of Lawrence have chosen to attend graduate school or professional school immediately after graduation. In addition, the workshops continue to provide a way to involve current students as teaching assistants, thereby increasing departmental esprit and pride and giving current students some ownership in the process of perpetuating the success and strength of the department.

> *Over 50 percent of the physics graduates of Lawrence have chosen to attend graduate or professional school.*

We were clearly pleased by this early progress, and shared news of these successes with others. Faculty members delivered reports on these undertakings at national meetings, and we hosted two conferences supported by the Sloan Foundation (one on laser physics in 1987 and one on computational physics in 1990) at Lawrence. Both conferences resulted in proceedings that were distributed gratis to all undergraduate physics departments in the country. Those efforts began to identify our physicists as innovators; they also left us with specialized facilities that remain to this day virtually unmatched in other small institutions.

Building a premier small physics department

But we did not stop there. Five years ago our physicists shifted their goal from developing specialties to creating one of the better small undergraduate physics departments in the country. Having figured out how they might attract a critical mass of good physics students, keep them interested, and help them seek careers in science and engineering, our physicists were emboldened to set about reinventing and revitalizing their department. After a good deal of consideration and debate, the physicists decided that the distinguishing characteristics of a premier small physics department include excellent teaching, a comprehensive curriculum, faculty research recognized elsewhere, an ample number of serious and able students actively learning physics and engaging in undergraduate research, and successful contributions to the institution and the external community through outreach efforts. They also convinced me that a premier physics department must nurture and challenge all students (majors and non-majors alike) with up-to-date facilities, excellent equipment, and a personal touch.

While good teaching and a solid curriculum are essential, the physicists were perhaps the first of our scientists at Lawrence to endorse the notion that a program is much more than a curriculum. They realized early on that for a department to improve itself, it had to give consider-

For a department to improve, it had to give attention to its entire program, not just to curriculum or to a few new teaching methods.

able attention to its entire program, not just to its curriculum or to a few courses or to a few new teaching methods. They envisioned a department that would provide students with strong backgrounds in theoretical, experimental, and computational physics and that endorsed a significant capstone activity in the senior year. They embraced the idea that each of the four faculty members would establish ambitious programs of research or scholarship that would complement their pedagogical efforts and lead to the creation of signature programs that would give the department a special identity, strengthen its capacity to recruit students, and provide the facilities and expertise for the offering of advanced elective courses. Currently, these areas of specialization within the department are experimental atomic and laser physics, computational physics, experimental condensed matter physics (specifically, liquid crystals, phase transitions, and X-ray diffraction), and experimental plasma physics focusing on non-neutral plasmas. New construction and renovation of a thirty-five-year-old building that is now taking place will provide each faculty member with a 500 sq. ft. research laboratory and a 750 sq. ft. laboratory space designed to support instruction associated with that faculty member's signature program.

The W. M. Keck Foundation was founded in 1954 by William Myron Keck, founder of the Superior Oil Company. Their grantmaking is focused on medical research, science, and engineering. The foundation also maintains a program for liberal arts colleges.

To implement their plans, our physicists—with some assistance from me as the road warrior on their behalf—set about to secure the needed support to develop facilities, to enhance their own expertise, and to undertake curricular innovation, efforts that together were aimed at bringing physics at Lawrence to a position of real distinction. Over the years, with proposals focused on strengthening many aspects of the enterprise, we approached the W. M. Keck Foundation, the National Science Foundation, the General Electric Foundation, the Pew Charitable Trusts, Research Corporation, the Sloan Foundation, and various other sources, assuring them that these projected developments at Lawrence would be pace-setting and would be disseminated widely in hopes of increasing the impact of their efforts and thus helping other institutions improve as well. In the last dozen years, success to the tune of $1.8 million in grants and gifts in kind, together with additional support from Lawrence, provided equipment and summer support for developmental and research efforts involving faculty and students.

Departmental development

While curricular developments and signature programs received primary attention in the late 1980s and early 1990s, our physicists more recently have focused greater attention and energy on faculty-student research and building departmental infrastructure. The governing principle here is the conviction that faculty engaged in original research stand a better chance of bringing the thrill of scientific discovery to their students. We all agree that ongoing involvement by science faculty in research or scholarship is critical to maintaining faculty viability, and that faculty commitments to independent research programs are necessary prerequisites to the support of undergraduate research. While this activity has existed at Lawrence for decades, we deemed its breadth and depth insufficient. Hence, with encouragement from Research Corporation, our physicists in 1994 crafted a four-year plan of departmental development that contained various elements (curricular development, library improvement, colloquium expansion, machine-shop improvement, etc.), the most pivotal of which was expanded research activity. Brandenberger, Cook and their colleagues felt that they needed four visible research programs on campus, and wanted to increase both their own productivity and that of the students involved in these programs.

Faculty engaged in original research stand a better chance of bringing the thrill of scientific discovery to their students.

After drafting several versions of such a plan and after a visit by President John P. Schaefer and former Vice-President Brian Andreen of Research Corporation, the physicists finally wrote a proposal that was awarded in 1995. Funds from a $300,000 grant from Research Corporation, matched by $250,000 from Lawrence and $400,000 from other sources over a period of four years have given our physicists the support to proceed much more broadly and systematically in their attempt to create a strong physics department. This effort during the past four years has involved annual visits to monitor the improvement of the program by consultants Robert C. Hilborn (Amherst College) and Robert B.

Hallock (University of Massachusetts, Amherst), as well as by Andreen and Michael P. Doyle of Research Corporation. The progress we have achieved through this five-year venture has been considerable.

A key element in this plan involved the hiring of a laboratory supervisor whose teaching of introductory laboratories made it possible for the four faculty members to devote greater time and energy to these developmental initiatives. One such initiative involves a new "capstone program" in which seniors, with considerable faculty assistance, pursue ambitious undertakings that usually assume the form of undergraduate research projects. These projects are substantial and substantive undertakings; they certainly rise above the level of "glorified homework," to quote a critical comment from an article by Leo Reisberg in *The Chronicle of Higher Education*[2] on this kind of work, even if they do not rise to the level of what Wernher von Braun had in mind when he quipped that research is "what I'm doing when I don't know what I'm doing." But these endeavors do enable our physics majors to do real science and to discover for themselves the joys as well as the frustrations entailed therein.

In addition to the capstone project, other programmatic improvements in the department include heightened research activities during both the summer and the academic year and a greater number of summer research opportunities for Lawrence students. Still another area of improvement involves outreach offerings designed to provide greater opportunities for non-majors to confront physics in various guises. Until recently, only occasional courses in the history of planetary astronomy, the history of motion, and the physics of music constituted special offerings by the department for non-majors. I am pleased that the physicists now offer a much broader range of outreach courses dealing with the nature of light, laser physics, the physics of music, relativity, cosmology, and astronomy. Some of these courses have laboratory components, and all are regularly elected by students seeking to fulfill the college's graduation requirement in science. These new offerings have proved popular, and some are already attracting overflow enrollments.

I might add that our physicists also have determined that engaging their students in an array of personal interactions is an invaluable component of a strong and vital program. Consequently, they hold twice-weekly teas in the departmental student lounge, get the students to help sponsor departmental open houses, organize weekend retreats for the entire department (all students and all faculty) at the university lodge on the shores of Lake Michigan, and encourage students to take advantage of the ready availability of faculty members outside of the classroom and laboratory.

Advice for departments

In October 1998, members of the department were invited to describe the results of these various efforts as a case study at a national meeting in Arlington, Virginia, sponsored by the American Association of Physics Teachers, the American Institute of Physics, the American Physical Society, the National Science Foundation, and Project Kaleidoscope. At that conference, entitled "Building Undergraduate Physics Programs for the 21st Century," our faculty members offered the following advice to physicists elsewhere who might be contemplating improvement of their programs:

- *Set ambitious goals, maybe even ones that appear at first unrealistic.* To provide motivation for significant improvement, such goals should be bold and broad; achieving them should require a stretch for the department.
- *Give attention to the entire program.* Efforts focused on curriculum alone (and certainly on only a few courses) constitute a start, but by themselves are insufficiently broad.
- *Make sure that the department develops a few features that are unique, that faculty members care about, and that are attractive to prospective students.* Such features in a departmental program are important to recruiting students, maintaining faculty enthusiasm, attracting new faculty, and obtaining outside funding.
- *Provide opportunities for student involvement in departmental affairs.* Students can, for example, contribute to curricular planning, interview candidates for positions, entertain visitors to the department, and assist with introductory laboratories and recruiting workshops. Regular social gatherings (e.g., frequent student-faculty teas, evening receptions for visiting scientists) and occasional large-scale events (annual retreats) can help nurture departmental rapport.
- *Make sure that students have an opportunity to interact with visiting scientists in the absence of local faculty.*
- *Cultivate challenging but simultaneously supportive relationships among students and between students and faculty.*
- *Strive for flexibility in the curriculum.*

- *Approach potential funding sources frequently and aggressively.*
- *Procure adequate space for the departmental program.* Classrooms, teaching laboratories, and offices are necessities, of course, but it is also important to seek spaces that students can call their own, research laboratories for faculty members, and laboratories for signature programs.
- *Develop effective methods for recruiting prospective students.* Recognize, though, that these efforts require substantial effort and will not succeed unless you have some excellence to underscore.
- *Aim at opportunities that will make a difference.* Our recruiting workshops are aimed at inducing those who have already applied to accept an offer of admission. While some students apply to Lawrence because of the opportunity to attend these workshops, the primary objective of the workshops is to generate acceptances of admission.
- *Strive for student involvement in research during both the academic year and the summer.* An effective component in our recruiting is having undergraduates tell prospective students about their personal projects.
- *Make sure that the development plan has broad support within the department and administration.* In hiring new faculty members, search for candidates who are likely to be team players.

The physicists at Lawrence—currently David Cook, John Brandenberger, Jeffrey Collett, and Matthew Stoneking—recognize that revitalizing a science program requires a great deal of work, that it must be carried out on several fronts, and that it cannot be done overnight. The enterprise requires a concentrated effort on the part of an entire department for perhaps five or ten years. Visible improvement may be a long time coming, but imagination and persistence pay off. Having seen how our physicists at Lawrence approach such an endeavor as a labor of love, I can attest to the pride and pleasure that they, the department, and the institution derive from their work. They tell me—and the evidence supports the claim—that the results of these initiatives have justified the effort. Not only have students and faculty come to Lawrence because of these commitments and achievements, they have stayed, and they and the college have flourished as a consequence. Æ

TIMELINE OF PROGRESS IN PHYSICS AT LAWRENCE

Significant events in physics at Lawrence during the past thirteen years include:

1986–87: Initial support for Brandenberger's pilot-project in laser physics is provided by G.E. and NSF. Sloan supports national conference on laser physics. Recruitment workshops launched for high school seniors interested in physics. Thirty percent matriculate, leading to a doubling of physics graduates. Department maintains two research programs supported by Research Corporation.

1988–1990: Keck Foundation and NSF provide grants for Cook's pilot project on computing in undergraduate physics. NSF Faculty Enhancement Workshops on laser physics offered. Support from Tektronix, NSF, Keck and Pew facilitates conversion of pilot projects to signature programs. Talks are delivered at conferences of the American Association of Physics Teachers (AAPT), Council on Undergraduate Research (CUR), American Association for the Advancement of Science, and Project Kaleidoscope, and at various universities. Three undergraduates conduct research during summer.

Department hosts Sloan Foundation conference on computational physics. Tektronix, DEC, Coherent, TMC, and Plexus support signature programs. Reports on pilot programs distributed nationally.

Twelve majors pursue undergraduate research during summer of 1991, and deliver talks at professional meetings. Department receives three NSF-ILI awards.

1991–92: Department graduates 13 majors, twice the previous average.

1992–93: Members of department serve in the American Physical Society (APS), CUR, and AAPT. Department sets goal to become a premier small physics department. Plan of action submitted to Research Corporation.

1994–95: Grants received from NSF-ILI, Research Corporation, Perkin-Elmer, and the Petroleum Research Fund. Second Keck grant supports computing and advanced lab. Four-year departmental award received from Research Corporation. Five students pursue summer research.

1996–97: Hiring of lab supervisor permits senior capstone program. Nine students pursue undergraduate research.

1998–99: Four recent graduates accept tenure-track faculty positions elsewhere. Department offers case study at meeting organized by AAPT, AIP, APS and Project Kaleidoscope. Lawrence breaks ground for molecular science building.

1999–2000: Department develops plan to add signature programs in plasma physics and surface physics. Lawrence's new science building completed and work begins on renovation of Youngchild Hall of Science.

Carrying out statistical surveys, or crunching numbers that have the undoubtedly unintended effect of making invidious comparisons between undergraduate and graduate institutions, are exercises that range from mildly interesting to pointless. The foolish dichotomies that pit undergraduate *versus* graduate institutions, research *versus* education, "faculty" research *versus* "student" research need to be retired once and for all. They are a divisive distraction that needs rapidly to be replaced with more substantive reflections on the central question of the drop in research activity at liberal arts colleges.

Robert L. Lichter is Executive Director of
The Camille and Henry Dreyfus Foundation.

ROBERT L. LICHTER

4 "RESEARCH IS IMPORTANT, BUT..."

IN THE PERIOD BETWEEN the late 1970s and mid-1980s, a group of undergraduate institutions repeatedly made the case that support for research at undergraduate institutions was a worthwhile endeavor. For much of the time before then, the only significant research-grant programs specifically directed to undergraduate institutions were the Petroleum Research Fund of the American Chemical Society, whose Type B grants began in 1957; and Research Corporation's Cottrell program, which began following World War II.

The growing interest in research culminated in a meeting at Oberlin College of the presidents of forty-eight small, private liberal arts colleges (LACs), self-designated as leaders in the sciences and known, strangely enough, as the "Oberlin 50" (see page 16). The resulting reports, which called for significant investment at LACs, dovetailed with a report (the "Neal Report") from the National Science Foundation (NSF) that called for attention to and investment in a broader array of issues in undergraduate science and mathematics education.

Together, the reports galvanized federal and private agencies directly and indirectly to create programs aimed explicitly at LACs. Thus arose the mammoth infusions of funds by the Howard Hughes Medical Institute (HHMI), the Pew Charitable Trusts, and the NSF through the Research Experiences for Undergraduates (REU) and Research in Undergraduate Institutions (RUI) frameworks. In the mid-1980s Research Corporation discontinued the only program it had for doctoral institutions so that it could increase its support of research in undergraduate institutions. In 1987, the Camille and Henry Dreyfus Foundation introduced what is now known as the Scholar/Fellow Program for Undergraduate Institutions (Appendix, page 189). As recently as 1993 and 1994, respectively, the Dreyfus Foundation

The HHMI was founded as a medical research organization in 1953 and began a grants program in 1987. The institute's Undergraduate Biological Sciences Education Program is intended to help strengthen undergraduate education and research in biology, chemistry, physics and mathematics.

Note: Opinions and viewpoints expressed in this chapter are solely those of the author.

introduced two more programs directed to undergraduate institutions, the Faculty Start-up Grant Program for Undergraduate Institutions, and the Henry Dreyfus Teacher-Scholar Awards Program. To a greater or lesser degree, other federal and private grantmakers also created new programs or broadened existing ones to embrace undergraduate institutions in general, and LACs in particular.

These programs arose in response to strong expressions of need and desire among those undergraduate faculty members who got the attention of their respective administrations and other champions of research with undergraduates. Grantmakers took the word of the faculty seriously because they believed in the central role of the faculty in academia.

"But we're a teaching institution"

Fifteen years after the Oberlin meeting, what is the status of research in liberal arts colleges? While a clear minority of exceptions can be identified, consider the following observations made during the last five years:

- Massive investment of hundreds of millions of dollars by federal and private grantmakers have had an unhappily minimal impact on the sustainability of a research thrust at LACs.
- The number of research publications from LACs has fallen.
- Research proposal submissions from—and hence awards to—LACs have at best remained flat.
- LAC faculty members are disproportionately underrepresented in research-related activities of professional organizations, and are disproportionately overrepresented in corresponding non-research ("educational") activities.
- LACs with identifiable research programs involving more than an isolated faculty member have stayed constant or diminished in number.
- Organizational advocates for undergraduate institutions have had limited success in promoting research.
- Science education reform efforts at undergraduate institutions ignore or make only passing reference to research.

What is going on? Why does a cluster of institutions, which in 1985 presented itself with great fanfare as the vanguard of research-based undergraduate science education, continue to clutch at that self-image despite strong evidence to the contrary?

Simply put, research is no longer the priority at LACs that its earlier proponents claimed and that many worked very hard to establish. Perhaps the best summary of the present situation is a comment made by a LAC dean during a recent discussion about research: "Research is important, but we're a teaching institution." The observations above suggest that the outlook this remark reflects has subtly worked its way more broadly into the structure of science education at small, private liberal-arts colleges.

Research is no longer the priority at LACs that its earlier proponents claimed.

Placing discussions into perspective

Research at LACs has been the subject of extensive discussion on the Internet and elsewhere, much of it constructive and thoughtful, some pointing fingers and assigning blame, some making excuses in the guise of citing reasons, and some challenging the very notion of research. More time and ink (electronic and otherwise) seem to be consumed discussing and debating what research is and is not, and how it should or should not be done, than is spent doing it.

It is important to put these and other such discussions, especially ones that emerge from the LACs themselves, into perspective. Their emphasis almost always is on the "selective" liberal arts colleges, those fifty to 100 who are "generally recognized as excellent," and of which the "Oberlin 50" were the first contingent. Almost always, the mea-

Baccalaureate-origin institutions of 1991-95 science doctorate recipients by Carnegie Classification* of U.S. institutions and field of doctorate [1]

	Total known Carnegie	Research universities	Doctoral universities	Master's colleges and universities	Baccalaureate colleges
Physical sciences, total	11,015	5,373	1,280	2,082	2,089
Chemistry	6,676	2,634	849	1,564	1,532
Physics and astronomy	4,267	2,692	425	511	549
Other physical sciences	72	47	6	7	8

**Research Universities* are the 125 leading universities in terms of federal financial support; *Doctoral Universities* are 111 doctorate-granting institutions; *Master's Colleges and Universities* (529 schools) offer a full range of baccalaureate programs and are committed to graduate education through the master's degree; *Baccalaureate Colleges* are 637 predominantly bachelor's-degree granting institutions that award 40 or more of their degrees in liberal arts fields.

sure of impact is the number of majors who ultimately complete doctorates in their major; or the inverse, the number of doctorate recipients who received their bachelor's degrees at LACs (the two measures are not identical).

Analyses based on this approach have several deficiencies. First, the selective LACs represent a minority of the universe of nondoctoral institutions, which number many more than 1,000 (more than 600 offer bachelor's degrees in chemistry alone). Thus, drawing numerical comparisons with doctoral institutions skews the results. If only a subset of undergraduate institutions, such as the selective LACs, is to be examined, then correspondingly only a subset of doctoral institutions should be selected as well. This, of course, raises the complex question of the criteria for selection.

Second, these analyses are based on accomplishments that have historical roots but may not accord with current realities. Leading and trailing reputational time constants are long. Many LACs are living off their historical assets at a rate faster than that at which they are being

Many LACs are living off their historical assets at a rate faster than that at which they are being replenished.

replenished. As noted above, recent annual reports of some highly reputed LACs reveals a disheartening drop in the commonly accepted indicators of research: publications and external grants. At the same time, another cluster of institutions has appeared well above the horizon: public undergraduate institutions, which display increases in both indicators.

Third, comparing the numbers of departmental majors who receive doctorates in the major with their departmental counterparts in universities overlooks the fact that universities have many more venues for undergraduates to pursue interests in science. In a large land-grant institution, for example, a student interested in chemistry might select from majors in chemistry, biochemistry, ceramic science, polymer science, chemical engineering, or agricultural chemistry. Many of those could pursue graduate study in the same graduate department.

Fourth, there is no question that figures may be manipulated in a variety of ways to show that disproportionate numbers of selective (but not all) LAC graduates historically have earned doctorates compared to the numbers of graduates in the entire academic universe. However, is that statistic the only measure of quality and success? Is it not at least as important to determine what the graduates—with or without doctorates—have actually accomplished? Should one not especially ask who have become leaders; who have made a difference, affected lives; indeed, who have changed lives? A comprehensive unpublished survey by this author demonstrates clearly that nearly 60 percent of winners of prestigious awards to young faculty in the chemical sciences—one measure of accomplishment—received their undergraduate degrees at doctoral institutions. The remaining 40 percent were divided nearly evenly between undergraduate institutions of all types and foreign institutions. Even when corrected for the *total* number of LAC graduates who received bachelor's degrees in the sciences, award winners come disproportionately from doctoral institutions. A similar survey of leaders in nonacademic settings would be worthwhile.

These observations are not intended to suggest, nor has it been suggested, that doctoral institutions are "better" than undergraduate institutions in general, or LACs in particular. Such a conclusion is just as fallacious as the claim by some advocates for LACs that they are "better" than doctoral institutions. Rather, the observations demonstrate the limitations of numerical analyses and the arbitrary purposes for which they can be used. Carrying out statistical surveys, or crunching numbers that have the undoubtedly unintended effect of making invidious comparisons between undergraduate and graduate institutions, are exercises that range from mildly interesting to pointless. The foolish dichotomies that pit undergraduate *versus* graduate institutions, research *versus* education, "faculty" research *versus* "student" research need to be retired once and for all. They are a divisive distraction that

The foolish dichotomies that pit research versus education, "faculty" research versus "student" research need to be retired once and for all.

needs rapidly to be replaced with more substantive reflections on the central question of the drop in research activity at LACs.

Multiple resources must be invested

Research requires investment of intellectual, physical and financial resources. The first two of these are not at issue. Undergraduate institutions teem with intellectual resources. The scholarship that does emerge can hold its own against any that comes from doctoral institutions, even if it appears at a necessarily slower pace. Many institutions, propelled by the largesse of the 1980s, have already invested in the physical plant, and others are continuing to do so. Indeed, rapidly rising endowments fed by a happy economic climate present infrastructure opportunities probably unmatched for nearly a generation.

What remains to consider, then, is garnering the financial resources necessary to carry out research and create scholarship. The evidence in recent years is that the common mechanism for doing so—preparation of competitive research proposals—has suffered a noticeable decline. "Proposal pressure"—I prefer "volume" to "pressure"—has dropped, especially in programs that are specifically directed to undergraduate institutions.

It is important not to be distracted by yet another numerical measure. Proposal volume is not the issue. A focus on research is presumably based on the premise that research is one of the most effective forms of learning, which in the end is the real value of research for all students, graduate and undergraduate. But, research costs money; proposals are a way to obtain money. Clearly, however, if institutions are willing to foot the entire bill in order to maintain even modest efforts, grantmakers can move on to use their finite resources for many other purposes where their constituencies have demonstrated a need. They would be irresponsible to do otherwise. That is another manifestation of the responsiveness principle that has led to creation of their programs in the first place. That much is obvious.

What is not obvious is why proposal volume is at best flat and what this means for the concept of undergraduate research as a mode of learning. That is where the discussion needs to go. Exhortations to write proposals have been ineffective and may even have a quality of blaming the victim. Even workshops on the mechanics of proposal writing are not a solution. Writing proposals is risky, exposing one's ideas for critical review and possible rejection is daunting. Rewards are perceived to be tenuous. Finding reasons—lack of time being the one cited most often—for not writing proposals or papers makes it easy to not address the heart of the issue.

What prices have to be paid financially, personally and institutionally in order to embed research into the institutional structure?

That issue is: what are faculty and institutional priorities and objectives? What is really important to faculty members *in their institutional settings*? If research is a significant part of the equation, what kind of framework needs to exist that fosters research? What prices have to be paid financially, personally and institutionally in order to embed research into the institutional structure? What changes will faculty members have to make and, especially, what time-honored practices might they have to give up, if any, in how they serve their students? These are some of the questions that have to inform the discussion.

In framing this issue, several points may be considered, First, there is a tendency, which has been articulated in a number of forums, to blame "the administration." That is a diversion. Academic institutions are complex organisms. Of the four academic components—students, faculty, administration (including support staff), and trustees (public or private)—the essence of academia resides with the faculty. The faculty is the glue that binds the institution together. Faculty members are the ones with the long-term institutional commitment, from whom emerges the intellectual substance of the institution. Where research is part of the academic intellectual contract, faculty members are the ones who add to new knowledge, to new interpretation of existing knowledge, or to other creative and artistic activities. They are the ones who drive the scholarship that arises from research and who ultimately, through the process of peer review and publication (or its artistic equivalent), characterize the value of that scholarship. As a result, it is the faculty that determines whether and how the students learn anything worthwhile.

> *Where research is part of the academic intellectual contract, faculty members are the ones who add to new knowledge.*

The faculty is as much a part of the institution as administrators. It can make things happen if it wants to badly enough. Administrators will respond if the faculty makes a compelling case for an outcome, and especially if it offers realistic pathways to reach that outcome, even if some negotiating has to take place along the way. Faculty members who have become senior administrators have already discovered this. Accordingly, the route to progress is not the intellectually shallow "us-*versus*-them" approach, but a true partnership—one in which each member brings something to the table—that articulates the relationship among research, teaching, and learning.

Second, the proposal review process, especially at federal agencies, is occasionally alleged to treat proposals from undergraduate institutions unfairly. Because the review process is a human one, it is inherently flawed. But NSF, for example, actively solicits new reviewers, which presents an opportunity for LAC and other undergraduate fac-

THE RESEARCH IN UNDERGRADUATE INSTITUTIONS PROGRAM

This NSF program encourages research by faculty members in predominantly undergraduate institutions both to ensure a broad national base for research and to help faculty stay at the cutting edge of their disciplines.

The RUI program supports high-quality research by faculty at undergraduate institutions, focuses on strengthening the research environment in academic departments that are oriented primarily toward undergraduate instruction, and promotes the integration of education and research. It funds individual and collaborative projects, the purchase of shared-use instrumentation, and supplemental awards for faculty to work with NSF-supported investigators at institutions other than their own. Unlike other NSF proposals, an RUI proposal must include a description of the effects of the proposed research on the research and educational environment of the institution.

ulty members to become reviewers, influence the outcome and possibly "educate" those who many feel block research support for undergraduate institutions. Reviewing proposals is also the best way to learn the subtleties of proposal preparation.

Third, and on a more practical note, LAC faculty members should realize that, while many private grantmakers have programs specifically targeted to undergraduate institutions, NSF's RUI (above and page 193) framework is not a program but a thrust that is embedded in the existing research directorates. No funds are specifically set aside for research in undergraduate institutions. NSF data suggest, however, that the success rates for proposals classified as RUI are the same as or better than those for proposals not so classified. The conclusion is inescapable: the barriers to support arise not at the funding agencies but within the faculty. More proposals are likely to lead to more funding.

Fourth, LAC faculty members often lament the lack of time available to write proposals, carry existing projects to completion, and develop new research areas, *in contrast to their counterparts at doctoral institutions*. Time is the currency of academia, and it is rarely fungible. LAC faculty members, however, are sadly misguided if they feel the amount of time in their accounts is under any more strain than is that of doctoral faculty members. The difference lies both in the distribution of purposes in which time is spent, and which of these purposes have priority. Doctoral faculty members are just as concerned as LAC

48

faculty members about meeting their administrative and service responsibilities to their institutions, spending time with families and friends, and devoting attention to nonacademic activities. They borrow or steal time wherever they can, especially evenings and weekends (see page 54). The stresses they feel are comparable, even if their origins differ from those of LAC faculty.

Fifth, the personal conflict some undergraduate faculty members feel between an emphasis on research and their allegiance to students has generated two misapprehensions. One is that the more research-oriented faculty members are less devoted to the academic development of their students than faculty members who are less research active. The dedication of these latter faculty members to their students is laudable, but they err if they assume, even implicitly, that undergraduate faculty members who choose to mount more-active research programs are not as passionate about the welfare and education of their students.

Can undergraduates do meaningful research?

The second misapprehension is that undergraduates are unable to do research in a meaningful way. In addition to buying into the bias accused of proposal reviewers from doctoral institutions, this implication runs the probably inadvertent risk of demeaning the many valuable scientific contributions that students and their faculty advisors have made to advancing scientific knowledge.

These attitudes, which attempt to assign responsibility elsewhere except within the faculty, are nonetheless a responsibility of the faculty to change. However, if undergraduate research at LACs is to return to and even surpass its earlier level, several additional contributions to a successful journey can be identified that can assist faculty:

An infrastructure that supports research. This does not mean merely equipment, start-up funds, laboratory space, and even internal research funding. Most of these are necessary but are hardly sufficient. Rather, it means building into the institutional fabric the expectation that scholarly activity—defined by the discipline—is prized as a means for faculty growth and student learning. It means that research is not merely added on to expectations of teaching and advising by faculty, but is an integral part of them. It means that research begins at the earliest feasible stages of a student's career, not

49

tacked on at the end as an afterthought. It means that the notion that teaching and learning—whether collaborative, cooperative, or

Research begins at the earliest feasible stages of a student's career, not tacked on at the end as an afterthought.

constructivist—take place primarily in classrooms and structured laboratories—a notion that has driven an enormous number of curriculum-reform efforts—has to be broadened to include research, not just rhetorically but palpably.

Perhaps one of the most counterproductive concepts in the realm of undergraduate research is the "capstone" research experience. The dictionary defines the capstone as the finishing stone of a structure. By contrast, expecting undergraduate research to be the pedestal on which the entire structure rests is unrealistic: undergraduates ought to be broadening their intellectual and creative limits in the widest possible manner. However, it does make sense to view research as a scaffold on which undergraduate learning is built, a framework that can embrace many areas.

Leadership. This means not just directives from the top (whose legitimacy is routinely, if not always appropriately, questioned), but energetic advocacy by the faculty, administrators, trustees, and other supporters of LACs, both within and outside the institution, for putting the infrastructure described above into place, and backing it up by judicious financial investment.

Heroism. This means that faculty members and administrators must be willing to take risks in sailing against the wind that depreciates research with students as an effective mode of learning *and* of advancing knowledge. It means thoughtfully and fundamentally questioning the inviolate wisdom that dictates faculty-student interactions at LACs (small classes, unlimited office hours, instant and constant faculty availability, for example), and aggressively inventing imaginative ways to ingrain research into achieving the same goals.

Standards. This means demanding that intellectual and scholarly accomplishments of the LAC faculty be of the same quality as those from any other setting; requiring proposals to be intellectually competitive with those from any other institutions; and expecting publications to undergo the same intensity of review as those from any other institution.

The notion of standards deserves a bit more exploration because it bears on the question of the drivers of faculty priorities and objectives.

Assuredly, granting agencies can make clearer that they are responsive to LAC proposals. Reviewers can be more generous in their assumptions about the feasibility of research projects in LACs. Leaders in the sciences—including some LAC faculty members—can stop dismissing research by undergraduates as "merely" education or, indeed, as a means primarily to foster faculty-student contact. Research is as much "education" for graduate students as it is for undergraduates, but no one thereby expects that graduate research will not advance the science.

Further, graduate students give papers and posters at scientific meetings in disciplinary and technical divisions, yet undergraduates are often relegated to sessions on "undergraduate research." This is as if they are doing research on undergraduates, as others do research in, say, organic chemistry. If undergraduate research is to be valued it needs to be held valuable *as research*, especially by the leaders of the scientific societies who set the tone for the validation given by the societies. Thus, it was disappointing to hear a president of a major scientific society suggest recently that an address by the faculty recipient of an award for research in an undergraduate institution be given in the society's education division rather than in the recipient's technical home. It is also for this reason that the recently advanced notion of a "Journal of Undergraduate Research" is particularly invidious if it is intended to be a venue for presentation of original research.

Leaders in the sciences can stop dismissing research by undergraduates as "merely" education or as a means to foster faculty-student contact.

All this means that the research has to be research: the creation of new knowledge (or new understanding of existing knowledge), its submission for critical review and community response by knowledgeable peers, and its public communication and presentation ultimately in archivable media. All components are necessary. Anything less may be a good pedagogical exercise, but it is not research. Calling it research will not make it so, and deceives students. Faculty members and undergraduates in doctoral institutions understand this. Many faculty members in undergraduate institutions do as well, but their numbers are dropping.

This situation could be ameliorated were an effective voice for research in undergraduate institutions to exist. It does not. Project Kaleidoscope, perhaps the most influential advocate for undergraduate

THE NATIONAL CONFERENCES ON UNDERGRADUATE RESEARCH

The idea for a national undergraduate research conference was conceived by chemist John Stevens at the University of North Carolina at Asheville, and its first conference was held there in 1987.

NCUR is committed to the promotion of undergraduate research and creative activity in all academic disciplines. Its primary outlet is the annual conference, held for two and-one-half days on a college or university campus. The first conference hosted 388 particpants, and since then as many as 2,449 have attended. The main function of the conference is to provide undergraduates with the opportunity to present their scholarly work, in oral or poster format, in an environment similar to that at professional conferences.

NCUR is administered by a twenty-four-member board which consists of representatives from educational institutions, industry and foundations. The board selects the host sites and provides oversight for the conference. NCUR's "home base" is Union College in Schenectady, N.Y.[2]

science education in general, has never stressed research in its mix of activities, its notions of "research-rich" curricula notwithstanding. The Council on Undergraduate Research has been such a voice, but needs to reexamine its priorities and activities so that it can reclaim its leadership position.

The organization with perhaps the greatest potential to be a voice for research in undergraduate institutions, as part of the larger framework of research by undergraduates, is the National Conferences on Undergraduate Research, NCUR (above). Through its annual conferences, NCUR has inspired thousands of undergraduates to seek out and participate in research across all disciplines, and has stimulated faculty members to rethink the ways in which research is carried out in their disciplines so that research projects appropriate for undergraduates can be created. Indeed, NCUR's successes have attracted multi-year foundation support for undergraduate research programs that include and, especially, go beyond the sciences.

Evidence of research accomplishment at undergraduate institutions does not differ from that at other institutions. Let us go back to the operational definition of research: new knowledge or understanding, presentation for critical review by experts, and publication in archivable media. The first component can take any number of forms, and while it does not matter in principle whether projects are student-originated or part of a faculty member's long-term effort, in fact the latter clearly will be more valuable. The excuse that

Evidence of research accomplishment at undergraduate institutions does not differ from that at other institutions.

students cannot get enough done in a summer to bring a project to completion is lame: nowhere is it written that research must be completed in discrete time units. Successful undergraduate faculty members divide larger projects into manageable chunks that ultimately are combinable into a publication of respectable quality.

The second and third components mean publication in peer-reviewed journals that persist over time, with all the attendant limitations and deficiencies. It does not mean oral presentations, although oral presentations are good learning tools, can build presentation skills, and can inspire the confidence to proceed with publication.

All components reflect the substance of scholarly accomplishment; however, they are not a measure of it. The pace of research at liberal arts colleges is necessarily slower than at doctoral institutions because the two types of institutions differ in the way their currency is spent. But the types of purchases with that currency—learning and scholarship—are the same.

All this requires a commitment to the enterprise of research. It means maintaining the "fire in the belly" that is the mark of committed scholars and dedicated teachers who take justifiable pride in their students and the contributions to knowledge and understanding, perhaps even to wisdom and enlightenment, that they make together. Then, one day, the successor to the dean quoted above might instead say, "research is important *because* we're an institution of learning." Æ

Time Management

Most of us have more demands on our time than we can possibly handle. How we respond to those demands determines to a great extent our effectiveness. Hence, the art of time management is one that busy professionals must master to succeed. In the words of Goethe, "things that matter most must never be at the mercy of things that matter least;" however, too often our attention is taken up with activities that are not productive.

A very attractive aspect of academic life is the flexibility we have, or are supposed to have, with our time. In academe there are also more—and more diverse—demands on our time than in many other careers. For example, in a typical week we may be asked to do something for the department head, for the dean, for students who need letters of recommendation, for the editor of a journal, for a federal grants review panel, for the recruiting office, for a newspaper reporter, and for the alumni association, to name a few. Often, after a few months on campus, an eager and enthusiastic assistant professor can feel so overcommitted that he or she becomes less and less effective. Because we are the only ones who know how many commitments we have, we are also the only ones who can remedy this. However, the pressures are such that change frequently comes only after a crisis.

I refer to time management as an art because no single formula applies to all cases, and any successful system must take into account individual styles and circumstances (suggested reading listed on page 196). Nevertheless, there are common elements worth noting.

- **Effective time management takes constant maintenance.** Not only do we need to define clearly the things that matter most to us, but we need to continually check our schedule and make sure it is helping us reach our goals.
- **Don't prioritize your schedule, schedule your priorities.** Weekly planning is something many of us do, or should do. In those weekly calendars we must first include the activities that will help us achieve our individual, family, and career goals. All other activities should come after these priorities are scheduled.
- **Choose quality over quantity.** External demands on our time tend to increase as we progress in our careers. Slowly but surely we notice that we cannot enjoy any of our tasks because we are chronically overwhelmed. By choosing to do fewer, more important, things and do them well, we will essentially be choosing excellence over mediocrity. Another important benefit of this choice is that we are likely to enjoy the process again, and not just the products.

The next time you start feeling like the white rabbit in Lewis Carroll's *Alice's Adventure in Wonderland*, repeating "Oh dear! Oh dear! I shall be late!" remember that you are not without alternatives. You can restore balance to your life and successfully meet your challenges without sacrificing your sanity. The means to achieving this healthy balance are within reach, the decision to use them is yours.

—Humberto Campins, Program Officer, Research Corporation

SECTION II

MODEL PROGRAMS

MANY SMALLER INSTITUTIONS HAVE,
IN THE PAST, CONTRIBUTED SCIENTISTS
OUT OF ALL PROPORTION TO THE
NUMBERS OF THEIR STUDENTS.

—"SCIENCE AND PUBLIC POLICY:
A REPORT TO THE PRESIDENT," 1947

THE CHALLENGE IS TO DEVELOP research programs for under-graduates in all colleges and universities that incorporate present, not past, methods. This requires creative interaction with industry, and more involvement with academic colleagues in marketing, man-agement, engineering, physics, materials science, law, and business-related fields. My prediction is that the undergraduate institution that takes unusual but creative real-world steps in developing cross-disciplinary, team-based research activities will take one giant leap over the competition in developing the undergraduate research paradigms of the next century.

Douglas C. Neckers is Director of the Center for Photochemical Sciences at Bowling Green State University.

Douglas C. Neckers

5 REMINISCENCES AND RECOMMENDATIONS ON UNDERGRADUATE RESEARCH

To the Memories of Gerrit Van Zyl and Harvey Kleinheksel—
Hope College Chemistry Giants in the Early Years

I AM A PRODUCT OF AN AMERICAN liberal arts college. So are my children, my wife, my parents, my brothers, their wives, my uncles and aunts, my grandfather and virtually everyone I know in the Neckers family. Over the course of a thirty-five-year career in science, I've been on boards, commissions, advisory committees and review panels that have punched, kneaded, investigated, probed, advised, and generally made nuisances of themselves to literally dozens of four-year colleges and their science faculties. Liberal arts colleges are in my blood. Hope College, my alma mater, was the only college I knew as a child and it defined for me what a college education was supposed to be.

Four-year colleges historically played a role disproportionate to their enrollments in the preprofessional education of scientists. This trend began to erode in the late 1960s lowering the accepted norms. The trends today are less certain but it would seem they are eroding still further, if the enrollment patterns in graduate programs in the physical sciences are any indicator. This is partially excused since fewer Americans have quantitative skills, and those who have them choose careers more lucrative than an industrial career in a laboratory science.

Worldwide political changes, as a result of the fall of the Soviet Union and the communist governments in the Soviet sphere of influence, and the opening of the borders of the People's Republic of China, have created an influx of brilliant students into the United States. An industrial career that looks pedestrian to an American honors student offers many foreign nationals orders of magnitude more in earning power than both their parents can earn collectively in their home countries. These two things together—careers that do not attract Americans and an influx of bright students from communist, and formerly communist countries—create incredible competition among graduate schools for the small number of native-born Americans who plan to enroll for graduate study.

Other trends also create an unstable, unsettling mix for careers in chemistry in American industry. Globalization and diversification of our

The Pimentel Report

The 1985 report by the National Research Council, *Opportunities in Chemistry,* was constructed by a NRC committee chaired by George C. Pimentel of the University of California, Berkeley.[1] This report, known widely as the Pimentel Report, stated "chemistry is a central science that provides fundamental understanding needed to deal with many of society's needs. . . . It is a critical component in man's attempt to feed the world population, to tap new sources of energy, to clothe and house humankind, to provide renewable substitutes for dwindling or scarce materials, to improve health and conquer disease, to strengthten our national security, and to monitor and protect our environment. Basic research in chemistry will help future generations cope with their evolving needs and unanticipated problems."

industries—soap companies that do not make soap, chemical companies that make no chemicals, and a merger mania that ensures only that no job is secure—are beginning to take their toll on the scientific workforce. In spite of every ACS president, past or present, repeating the Pimentel Report's dictum that chemistry is the central science (see above), the fact is students are more attracted elsewhere. Unless there is some significant restructuring and focus, undergraduate research in chemistry departments, mostly built on a scientific model of the 1970s, will become even less relevant than it is now. Americans want a healthy citizenry and industries that fuel the world's greatest economy. The challenge for academic scientists is to help our citizens achieve that goal.

In the last four decades, scientific research has become increasingly more complex. Years ago, a research problem was between a student and faculty mentor. Solving problems now requires teams of scientists, each with different yet highly-honed skills, working together to achieve one common objective. The old model—a single investigator working with a student or two—may be the easiest pedagogy to practice, but it is less and less relevant to real-world research situations. The challenge is to develop research programs for undergraduates in all colleges and universities that incorporate present, not past, methods. This requires creative interaction with industry, and more involvement with academic colleagues in marketing, management, engineering, physics, materials science, law, and business related fields. My prediction is that the undergraduate institution that takes unusual but creative real-world steps in developing cross-disciplinary, team-based research activities will take one giant leap over the competition in developing the undergraduate research paradigms of the twenty-first century.

Looking backward to see the future

But let's look backward to see the future. I spent from 1964 to 1971 teaching at Hope College. When I started my laboratory career, four-year institutions literally had no research instruments. What I had the pleasure of doing was helping my alma mater enter the post-Sputnik generation in chemistry.

Hope is a college of the Reformed Church in America located in Holland, Michigan, a part of the United States that is as conservative, religiously and politically, as any in the country. The area is also prosperous. In a recent survey of largest American privately held companies, seven of the top 500 were located in just two Michigan counties, Ottawa (where Hope is) and nearby Kent (Grand Rapids). Most are manufacturers of products like furniture, some still handcrafted by artisans. Others are marketing oriented. Buy low, sell high, and outwork the competition. Research and development in these companies is product-driven. There's a lot of reverse engineering. Find someone else's product, take it apart, and put it back together again under your label. Citizens of the area run the Michigan Republican Party and speak with great gusto about the evils of the federal government. Nevertheless, each year when the federal largesse is handed out, those companies who propound less government benefit well beyond their taxable contributions in federal return to their enterprises.

Undergraduate research played a major role not only in my choosing to be a chemist, but specifically in my choosing to be an organic chemist. During my junior year in college, Gerrit van Zyl, who was head of Hope's chemistry department, invited one other student and me to spend the subsequent summer working on a research project. I had spent most of my previous summers either working in my dad's general store or on a construction project making money for the next year's tuition. The idea of doing something that seemed more like fun than work appealed to me even though the pay was next to nothing. What's more, I couldn't imagine why anyone would pay me to work in the lab.

Van Zyl wasn't around much. About the only time we saw him was on Friday afternoons when he would deliver our weekly $50 paycheck. Our programs were self-directed. Two senior students, one of whom was Vic

Heasley, professor of chemistry at Point Loma Nazarene College since 1963, directed my project. I was totally inept in the laboratory, and barely managed not to injure myself (though I could have) or harm my colleagues (I could have done that too). Nevertheless, the experience was the most interesting of my young academic life, and I found a career path as a result. Before that summer work had been work, and fun had been fun. Suddenly, that all changed. Work in a lab was fun and offered me the potential of making a living. This was an incredible revelation.

"Change the place"

I got into teaching more or less by accident. My uncle was a professor of chemistry and my mother a high school English teacher, so I decided there was nothing wrong with teaching school for a living. Much more important at that time, however, was that teaching was what many I admired did for a living. It had to be a good career if so many fine people were doing it.

So I chose teaching chemistry. It is actually more accurate to say teaching chose me. In 1962, while I was a doctoral student at the University of Kansas in Lawrence, Calvin A. VanderWerf, chair of the chemistry department, announced he would leave there to become Hope's seventh president. One day Cal called me to his office and asked if I would like to return to Hope to teach when I finished my degree. I'd never thought of such a thing, but was sincerely flattered by the invitation, so I told him I'd seriously consider the notion.

Cal was a wonderful president. At that time, the college was an institution primarily known for educating the sons of Dutch immigrants to be either chemists or preachers. As a university scientist, President VanderWerf brought Hope recognition of the value of research as a teaching tool. A highly esteemed educator, he was well aware of the pitfalls associated with too much emphasis on research. Cal was also a Hope graduate. His goals were to turn his alma mater into a place where research augmented undergraduate teaching and make the school one of the best in the country. His objective was that the Hope College lead the way in creative instruction at the undergraduate level. Thirty-seven years later it seems apparent that he accomplished many of his goals.

As I considered the offer to teach at Hope, I realized there were several years of research work I would have to do with my own hands, no matter where I was, so I might as well do it at Hope where I felt at home.

Hope had not benefited, as had other institutions, from the tremen-

Gerrit van Zyl, appointed in 1923, was Hope's first Ph.D. chemistry professor.

dous growth in undergraduate populations as a result of the post-war and Sputnik booms. Its undergraduate enrollment had actually decreased over the several years between 1960, the year I graduated, and 1964, the year I returned there to teach. This was clearly worrisome, and the president had to do something about it quickly. One of the things Cal did was to give his young faculty the freedom to "change the place." An influx of young assistant professors who saw teaching as a career, and research an essential part of it, forced dramatic changes on the institution.

As it turns out, it was a distinct pleasure working in a faculty where Cal VanderWerf was the senior academician. No individual I've ever met respected the academy more than he, and few I've known held the responsibility of the professorate in greater awe. These years were most valuable at a formative time in my career, and I'm grateful for them.

Hope's first chemistry teacher, Almond T. Godfrey, was a local physician. GerritVan Zyl, who had been at the college since 1923, was the first Ph.D. chemist to teach at the school. Though he had taught organic chemistry for most of his career, Van Zyl's degree was in physical chemistry. Ironically, though Hope based its reputation on the performance of its chemistry majors—most of whom became organic chemists—Jerry Mohrig and I (hired in 1964) were actually the first organic chemists to teach there.

61

In retrospect, what was taking place at Hope in the mid-60s was also happening in other colleges around the United States. The generations that had been lucky enough to get college and university teaching jobs before World War II were retiring. These dedicated people had nobly survived the depression, often giving up some of their salary so their institutions could remain open. By the early 1960s, however, a new era dawned, and hidden in its *eos* were young scientists who not only were happy to have teaching careers but thought doing chemistry or physics was fun. For them science, not *the* college or college teaching for that matter, was the career choice. The new generations expected to be creative, practicing scholars even at predominantly undergraduate institutions. Faculty in liberal arts colleges, particularly in the sciences, would soon be expected to find external funding and support students with their efforts just like their university counterparts.

Two cultures

It is not surprising to me now, but when I started my teaching career, I was completely unprepared for the existing liberal-arts-college persona. Many on the campus ignored creative scholarship, or had attitudes toward it diametrically opposed to those of academicians I so deeply respected. There were endless discussions about general education and what it really meant to have a liberal arts degree. The sciences, which represented the chosen majors of nearly 20 percent of the undergraduates studying at Hope in those days, were largely ignored in the general education mix. The basic curriculum contained too little science to be meaningful.

The basic curriculum contained too little science to be meaningful.

The fact that Hope's reputation was largely built based on its chemistry programs also led to an intense enmity between C. P. Snow's two cultures.[2] Colleagues who fancied themselves educated were proud to admit they knew no science, and pretentiously insulted those of us who were scientists by feigning an inability to understand even when we tried hard to explain what we were doing in simple terms.

To give the devil his due, the scientists themselves did not do much to aid the cause. The courses they offered to non-science students were mostly the same courses the science majors took, and the lower level courses were then—as now—pretty boring.

There were also endless discussions about where research fit in an undergraduate institution (see insert, page 63). I hadn't thought about

SCHOLARSHIP RECONSIDERED

The wisdom of research in undergraduate curriculum continued to be questioned for many more years. In 1990, *Scholarship Reconsidered* by Ernest Boyer extended the debate with a directly opposite viewpoint:[3]

Even institutions that enroll primarily undergraduates—and have few if any resources for research—seek to imitate ranking research centers. In the process, their mission becomes blurred, standards of research are compromised, and the quality of teaching and learning is disturbingly diminished. "By believing themselves to be what they are not . . . ," as Ernest Lynton and Sandra Ellman of the University of Massachusetts put it, "institutions fall short of being what they could be" and, in the process, not only deprive society of substantial intellectual services, but also diminish the vitality of higher learning.

this much since it seemed to me that teaching and research must be symbiotic, even at a four-year college. It's a noble profession, the professorate, and virtually any individual entering it cherishes its basic set of values. Though mainly a secure life, and one in which the practitioners have a striking degree of personal independence, most faculty members are conscientious and dedicated. This is particularly the case when it comes to doing the best for the students. Virtually no day goes by in most departments and institutions in which faculty do not discuss, worry about, delight in, consider the options, or in some other way think together about what's best for the students. It seemed pretty clear to me that in the academy a good teacher is a combination of instructor, mentor, cheerleader and coach whose role is to lead others to a deeper understanding through practice, criticism and analysis. As a practical matter, to be a scientist one had to be able to carry out scientific experiments at some level. It also seemed obvious to me that to teach science, I also had to carry out creative scientific experiments. What's more, I needed to teach my students how to do that also. If they were anything like I was as an undergraduate, they would love the opportunity.

But there are always temptations and ways for faculty to otherwise bide their time, and perhaps that was what the discussions were about. In the four-year liberal arts college, where there are no graduate students to force one to be continually at the intellectual forefront, it becomes particularly difficult to remain current over the course of a career. The addition of the NSF Research in Undergraduate Institutions (RUI; page 193), and the NIH Academic Research Enhancement Award (AREA; page 135) programs in the 1980s improved this, but the temptation to fall behind remained, particularly in the smaller schools.

Publish or perish?

As a new assistant professor at Hope, I quickly tired of the incessant backbiting and gossip which seemed particularly offensive in a non-Ph. D.-granting institution. Most of this at Hope was targeted at a president who was changing things. Although Hope was also my alma mater, I knew that unless the catholic campus environment underwent a reformation, I'd have no interest in staying there. I avoided the conflict(s), at least in my first few years, by trying to mind my own business. Without really recognizing what I was doing or starting, I transferred an enthusiasm for my own undergraduate research experience to a corporate, departmental culture in the early 1960s that remains at Hope, perhaps more than at other liberal arts colleges, to this day.

I wasn't responsible for this alone, nor did I start it. Van Zyl started it; VanderWerf encouraged it; and my colleagues in chemistry subscribed to it enthusiastically. However, I was the youngest faculty member in chemistry at Hope in the mid-1960s, had no children at the time, and was driven to achieve a research career of my own. So I provided much of the energy.

I rationalized my commitment to undergraduate research in a number of ways. "Students learn chemistry best by doing chemistry as chemists do it" was the way I wrote it in the first edition of the Mohrig and Neckers organic chemistry laboratory textbook.[4] In reality, my own objectives were also less pure. An academic career in chemistry in the '60s was dead in the water in the absence of research productivity, so publish or perish it became. Regardless of the attitudes of faculty in the humanities at Hope, research work was the way I practiced my trade so I intended to keep doing it. After all, half of the faculty in other departments were licensed clergy, and most all of them spent most every Sunday preaching in one or another of the churches around western Michigan. The music faculty saw nothing untoward about singing at weddings and funerals, or directing church choirs and getting paid for doing so. What was the difference? Thus driven, we made "undergraduate research" a mantra for all the sciences at Hope and it was transferred, through Mike Doyle and others, to many four-year schools across the country in the years immediately following.

Instruments and library resources

Most of the better liberal arts colleges at the time talked about research just as they still do today, but I had another idea in mind. It was eminently clear that if faculty in liberal arts colleges were going to maintain currency, they would have to do so as practicing scientists, not just as teachers of science. To a greater or lesser degree, that meant one had to bring a university-like mentality to young faculty in the liberal arts institution, at least at Hope. As far as I was concerned, this was the only way for faculty in these institutions to maintain a modicum of respect as the academy moved to academic attitudes driven by the huge influx of federally-funded research programs.

One had to bring a university-like mentality to young faculty in the liberal arts institution.

Fortunately, getting my own research program started was relatively easy since my equipment needs were modest. It was a good thing, because I never considered the idea that one might ask for start-up funding. The Hope I knew operated on a shoestring. As I recall, the cost of my entire start-up package (a bottle of D_2O and two microdistillation rigs) was less than $100. I knew that I needed a working gas chromatograph, the simpler the better, an infrared spectrometer and a vacuum pump in order to accomplish anything in the lab. Though Hope had reasonable facsimiles of such things, most of them didn't work.

Chemistry itself was at the threshold of the instrument generation so it was just a matter of time before Hope, and other liberal arts colleges too, would have to assemble a cadre of basic, but expensive, research instrumentation in order to survive academically. Fortunately, this was recognized by the funding agencies, at least somewhat. Van Zyl had received a modest NSF equipment grant during the last year or so before he retired and used it to purchase a few basic instruments. In a back office I found a new gas chromatograph, but it was of obsolete design and had been sold to Van Zyl by an unscrupulous equipment salesman presumably as a bargain. So a critical issue became assembling the instruments for simple research in organic chemistry.

Irwin Brink was chairman of the department at the time and during my first year of teaching taught me an important lesson about being a good department chairman: Irwin overran his operating budget in January. (I tried hard to emulate his good example each and every year of my twenty-three-year tenure as chemistry chair at Bowling Green.) One thing that aided and abetted Irwin's running the department budget out of money that year was that he bought me a new gas chromatograph with which to begin my work. By June I had completed enough work for my first independent publication. It was a short communication, and a derivative of my Ph.D. dissertation, but it proved the point—at least to me: I could establish an independent research career at a liberal arts college as well as anywhere. I then set about transforming Hope into a place where scientific research careers need not take a back seat to any in the academic community of scholars.

I could establish an independent research career at a liberal arts college as well as anywhere.

Fortunately, since the president was a chemist, I had his help, probably without his knowing it. When I went to see the college librarian and told him that our collection of journals in chemistry was woefully inadequate, he said "The president's a chemist, and I'm not going to worry about my budget; tell me what you need." So my colleagues and I put together a list.

I don't remember everything I put on the list, but the Hope chemistry library was woefully inadequate. We added the Royal Society journals, German journals and all the new issues sold by Pergamon Press at that time. The Hope library, unless it's been reorganized in recent years, can still trace the evidence of those many journals in chemistry whose subscriptions I arranged for the department starting in 1964.

Wooden shoes

Our chemistry faculty numbered six in 1964, and meetings consisted of an hour or so in Irwin Brink's office. At one meeting in the early fall Irwin said "We have these letters from university faculty wanting to come here and give talks. Should we do something about them?" So we started a regular seminar program.

Cal VanderWerf was fond of pointing out that "university faculty need the liberal arts colleges more than college faculty need the universities." So we coupled this to another VanderWerf budget principle "Always travel on the other guy's coin." We made it clear to university faculty that they could come see us if they liked, but it was at their expense. We gave them lunch, the pleasure of our company and, if they had to stay overnight, dinner. Analytical chemistry faculty member, Dave Klein, decided we should do more than that. So, he sent the science division's part-time secretary(!) to a local wooden-shoe factory with copies of the signatures of each member of the chemistry department. The secretary had the carver inscribe all of our signatures on a fancy pair of wooden shoes, and keep our signatures for future reference. Sometime in 1964–65 we began a tradition that exists to this day—every Hope seminar speaker gets his or her very own pair of wooden shoes. By 1967–68, when I ran the program, Hope's seminar series included more winners of ACS national awards than any seminar program in the country, and all it cost us was a few lunches and several $4 pairs of Dutch *klompen*.

Waiting for the money: NSF, PRF and ARO

Hope's first Undergraduate Research Participation (URP) proposal was written in 1964–65. Actually Dave Klein wrote it and Jerry Mohrig became the first principal investigator. As a faculty we argued incessantly over the details until all of us could sign off on the proposal. I remember Jerry Mohrig announcing at one of our meetings in Irwin Brink's office that he had sent our proposal to NSF well ahead of the deadline date, and that all we had to do now was wait for money. Imagine our shock and his chagrin and embarrassment when a letter later came from Washington "We regret to inform you that . . . ."

At Cal's instigation, Jerry called the NSF program director, took some notes about why the proposal had been turned down, made the few minor changes suggested in time for the next deadline, and this time the proposal was funded. I imagine that Hope's Research Experiences for Undergraduates (REU) program in chemistry has now been funded for more years than most any in the country, but it started with our URP proposal in 1965.

All of us also had small individual grants. Cal was on the Petroleum Research Fund (PRF) Board of Advisors at the time and had been particularly insistent that PRF set up a program to help young faculty get started. He anticipated that faculties were to grow rapidly as a result of the post-Sputnik boom, and wanted to be sure younger faculty got the best possible chance to develop creative careers. With his and Paul Bartlett's (my post-doctoral adviser) enthusiastic support, PRF initiated the Type G program for young faculty in 1964 (page 178). Jerry Mohrig and I were among the recipients of the first round of grants. As I remember, the award amount was $2,000. Cal bragged to all who would listen that Hope College was the only institution in the country with two young faculty who had successfully applied for PRF Type G funding. This was followed, for me, by a succession of Type B grants and later Type AC funds that eventually terminated after my program was funded by NSF and other granting agencies. But that was years later.

In spite of rather modest successes, grantsmanship at Hope, and in those days of the liberal arts colleges in general, was an intimidating challenge. I can't tell you how many times program officers at NSF and the defense agencies patted me on the head and said: "Forget it boy. Research is for graduate institutions. You can't do competitive work with undergraduate students." Nevertheless, I kept applying for major funding and eventually succeeded in getting a NSF grant and a fellowship from the Alfred P. Sloan Foundation at the time I was leaving Hope.

One occasion I recall involved a proposal I submitted to the Army Office of Research (ARO). Ted Oegema, now a distinguished professor in biochemistry at the University of Minnesota, and I had discovered some interesting thermal reactions of thiols with aromatic azo compounds. Since one could make bombs from compounds containing nitrogen-nitrogen double bonds, I reasoned the Army should be interested in supporting some further investigations of these systems. So, I wrote a letter of inquiry. When the response from the program officer was enthusiastic, I submitted a proposal and asked VanderWerf, a senior scientist, to join me as a co-investigator to give my effort credibility. Several months later the program officer expressed detailed interest, wanted to arrange a site visit, and came to see us a few weeks later.

I thought we had a very good visit. He told me that I had an excellent proposal and that it looked like it would be funded. As the afternoon wore on he also told me he had a sister in the town of Holland with whom he would be spending the weekend.

When, a couple of weeks after his visit, I got the standard "We regret to inform you . . ." letter, I called him to ask why and he gave me the typical "undergraduate only, four-year liberal arts college" response. "Our advisory board thinks you cannot accomplish such ambitious objectives in a four-year college environment." I suspect now that he was just leading me on, and a visit with his sister was the primary reason for his trip.

That experience aside, until the set-aside programs of the 1970s, funding for serious research in four-year institutions was next to impossible to get. There were, however, other ways to skin a cat. One example is how we managed to fund an NMR spectrometer at Hope by approaching goverment agencies and a local chemical manufacturer (see "The First Spectrometer at Hope," page 165).

Curriculum revision

Hope's chemistry department also began growing at that time. The Great Lakes College Association (GLCA) obtained funds from the Kettering Foundation to attract bright young scientists in chemistry and biology to liberal-arts teaching careers. As part of this program, Hope hired a biologist, Al Brady. In chemistry we used the funds to start offering legitimate courses in biochemistry, since among the earlier GLCA-initiated hires in the chemistry department was Hope's first full-time biochemist. We—mainly physicist Dick Brockmeier and I—also wrote a proposal to the Alfred P. Sloan Foundation to revise the basic science curriculum. This proposal came at the foundation's invitation and, when it was awarded, became the largest single grant Hope had ever received. Brockmeier, also a Hope alumnus, had taken his Ph.D. in physics at Caltech where he had become exposed, possibly on its first offering, to Richard Feynman's undergraduate course.[5]

Dick Brockmeier was an incredible visionary and a man whose insights I sincerely appreciate now that I've had a chance to live a life in science. In writing that Sloan proposal, Dick encouraged the institution to develop an undergraduate science curriculum that was both ahead of its day, and quite beyond the reach of both the faculty and the students when we tried to put it in practice. Dick's idea was that every Hope freshman had to qualify in calculus in order to take freshman courses in chemistry and physics. The first course in chemistry should be a one-semester introduction to the principles, followed by a second semester of organic chemistry. Freshman physics would be taught to science majors concurrently and begin with the principles of quantum mechanics. The culmination of all this would be the penultimate and ultimate courses in molecular biology. If, according to Dick, we did it right, most Hope science graduates would seek advanced degrees in biochemistry or molecular biology which were, after all, to be the way of all science in the future. These fields would, of course, also be far better off because those entering them would be molecular scientists, not ecologists or anatomists.

In fact, the curriculum Dick conjured up was a brilliant stroke, but one that put course content a bit beyond the reach of the average Hope freshman. For about the first and only time in my career, I began to see my name taken in vain on the bathroom walls, because it fell to Mike Doyle and I to teach organic to second semester freshmen. As I recall there were about 180 students in the class, so this was also my first real exposure to mass instruction. The curriculum was tremendously labor-intensive, so Brockmeier and our Sloan curriculum both bit the dust in just a few years.

But the influx of funds from the Sloan Foundation let us do things we hadn't been able to do before, like start a geology department and add

F. Sheldon Wettack (left) and student at Hope College in 1972.

faculty in physics. Coupled with a grant from Research Corporation we increased our chemistry faculty to nine full-time members. I don't remember exactly in what order this occurred but eventually Dwight M. Smith, F. Sheldon Wettack, and Michael P. Doyle were added to our eclectic six.

Wettack's credentials surfaced in a search for a physical chemist when, as I recall, Irwin Brink said in a faculty meeting "we should really take a look at this guy from Texas." He was the last Ph.D. student of W. Albert Noyes, Jr. Wettack, who had studied at San Jose State to be a high school chemistry teacher, somehow found his way to Texas as part of a summer institute for high school chemistry teachers. There he encountered Noyes, the former editor of the *Journal of the American Chemical Society,* and decided to stay on for a Ph.D. degree. His degree completed, Sheldon faced the dilemma of deciding between a postdoctoral position and an eventual university teaching career, or seeking a teaching position in institutions which would hire him with no postdoctoral experience. It took much convincing and incredible start-up funds for those times—$40,000—but eventually Sheldon came to Hope as an assistant professor.

Grantsmanship

The Alfred P. Sloan Foundation awarded twenty grants to liberal arts colleges in 1966. The foundation's motivation was to provide funding for the smaller schools—which it recognized for their roles as feeder institutions—to remain competitive in the then current academic environment. Carleton College also received funding from the foundation. Sometime during the subsequent year, Jerry Mohrig told me he was visiting Carleton for a day, and a week or so later he announced he was going to leave Hope after the spring semester of 1967 for a position there. Later, Dick Ramette, head of the Carleton chemistry department, visited Hope to lecture in a summer institute for high school teachers that Gene Jekel directed from the early 1960s until he retired in the 1990s. At lunch, we talked about the Sloan grant, and Dick told us something I used to great advantage many times later in my career. Sloan, in their letter of invitation to the small colleges, had said proposals would be accepted from individual institutions for "up to a maximum of a one-time grant for $500,000." Ramette said the proposed budget Carleton submitted to Sloan was for $565,000—$65,000 beyond the suggested maximum. Brockmeier and I worked very hard on Hope's proposal, carefully constructed a budget, and the total came to $375,000. So that's what we requested. When the awards were announced, we got our requested $375,000 and Carlton got the maximum—$500,000.

Thus, a principle of grantsmanship was indelibly reinforced by a simple luncheon with a more experienced fund raiser. Afterwards, at least as far as departmental proposals were concerned, we would "always ask beyond the maximum" if we really wanted the maximum. It is a dictum I used continually, and to great advantage, during my career as department chair at Bowling Green.

Advice to fund raisers: "Always ask beyond the maximum."

Anyway, Sloan funded Carleton, Carleton hired Mohrig, and I was stuck with finding a replacement or carrying the organic teaching load myself. As strange as that may seem to my current colleagues, that's exactly what I did for a year, but I did it for a very good reason. That reason was Mike Doyle.

Further reflections

We placed the usual ads in *Chemical and Engineering News* for an organic chemist, and I called former Harvard colleagues most of whom were now in university teaching positions. Columbia's Nick Turro said his people, Gary Schuster, Fred Lewis, Chris Dalton and others, were all heading for university positions. Mike McBride, at Yale, was talking with

Michael P. Doyle and chemistry students at Hope College in 1972.

someone in his office when I reached him and he asked that other person about potential candidates. The person must have asked McBride "What kind of place is it?" McBride, himself an alumnus of the College of Wooster, said, "OK, I guess. Neckers went there." Flattery got me nowhere though, because no candidates surfaced from Yale. Larry Singer, then at Chicago recommended a student of Tom Kaiser's and, after an interview, we eventually hired him for one year.

But Walt Trahanovsky at Iowa State told me about this guy he had— Mike Doyle. I don't remember all the details of the conversation but do remember Walt saying that a smaller school, like Hope, would be best for Doyle. He expected him to be a good teacher, and knew that undergraduate students would really like him. Besides, Walt told me, "Doyle has almost boundless energy."

So we set about interviewing several candidates for the organic chemistry job. The pool, in retrospect, was incredibly strong and a number of persons we didn't interview have gone on to successful careers in liberal arts colleges. But we did interview three, and Doyle was one of them.

Hope was typical of many church-related liberal arts colleges of the day. It had relatively strict religious criteria that were applied to all potential faculty. Since it was a College of the Dutch Reformed Church (later Reformed Church in America) it preferred preachers of that ilk as faculty members. When none showed up in the search, any other preacher would do. Only when no clergy applied would a Protestant of the right academic persuasion be considered. Mike fit none of those criteria so it took a while to convince the powers that be that he was "OK," and we eventually hired him. A year after our search was first began, Mike joined the faculty in an appointment that has probably been more important to liberal arts-college science than any in American history.

But by this time, my days at Hope were drawing to a close. I had finished my first research years and was eager to take the next steps in my own career. I was also growing incessantly sick of campus politics and the small town. President VanderWerf was under increasing criticism from the church and from the humanities faculty.

So, as Doyle was arriving, I arranged a leave in the Netherlands where I got a chance to develop some of my own ideas, learned some new research techniques, and met some people who would become lifelong friends. American politics had moved from the docile time of the early 1960s, accelerated by the assassination of President John F. Kennedy, to the confrontational period of Vietnam. Students, with whom I had worked closely, were getting draft numbers that made it certain they would end up in some far off place in harms way. The campus, like all campuses, was upset with itself and with its country. There was substantial community-campus tension brought on by a conservative western Michigan political outlook. And I had moved, philosophically and artistically, well away from the Reformed Church in which I had grown up.

In 1971, I left for the University of New Mexico. Almost immediately after arriving in Albuquerque, I began discussions with Bowling Green State University and, for all intents and purposes, moved there as chair of the chemistry department almost directly from Hope in the fall of 1973.

A look back

It's easier for me now to assess my years at Hope and in the liberal arts college community from a distance of years. I was young, impetuous, and impatient, and the general persona of the Hope I joined in 1964 was shop-worn and tired. My colleagues in chemistry, particularly Irwin Brink, Gene Jekel, and the late Harvey Kleinheksel, were incredibly patient with the my youthful arrogance and my peccadilloes. I did my job and did it well, if indeed the job was to change the coming generations in chemistry at the institution. For sure, those several years in the 1960s set the direction of a path in the sciences from which it never retreated. The real credit belongs to the VanderWerf administration and Cal personally. Not only did his presidency instigate changes in chemistry, but biology and physics became incredibly strong as result of initiatives begun during his administration. The college competed successfully for its own Phi Beta Kappa chapter (Cal was its first, and only, honorary member), purchased its first computer, and in many ways, placed itself on the road toward academic strength and excellence that it, and the region, have significantly benefited from to this day. But what I learned most from Cal was in what high regard he held the academic profession. No one I've ever met knew the university better or respected it more than Cal. He was a real role model.

Though I'm sometimes critical of Hope College, I also benefited from teaching there in a number of ways. Some of the lessons I learned from my undergraduate research associates stand with me to this day. One of these was that students could be good lab observers. When a result I found puzzling caused me to send a student back to do the experiment over again, the student maintained he was right and that I needed to change my theory. Several Hope undergraduates, during the early days of the Vietnam War, kept questioning why I was insisting they do this experiment or that.

The student maintained he was right and that I needed to change my theory.

"What's that good for?" they asked. When I discovered I could not tell them, I decided it was time to change the research problems on which I was working. The result, eventually, was a career in polymer photochemistry from which my main research reputation developed. Others taught me while they learned themselves. Some of my most satisfying academic experiences have been those occasional situations in which relatively minor comments made out of concern for a young person's well-being made differences in young people's lives.

The people we hired at Hope during those formative years have not done badly either. Wettack became president of Wabash College and is now executive vice president and dean of the faculty at Harvey Mudd College. Dwight Smith became president of the University of Denver. Dave Marker, in physics, became president of Cornell College in Iowa. Jerry Mohrig became a distinguished professor at Carleton. Mike Doyle was a distinguished professor at Trinity University before moving to Research Corporation.

On the national level, Doyle, almost single-handedly, started the

Douglas C. Neckers explains the operation of an NMR spectrometer to Bowling Green students (ca. 1977).

Council on Undergraduate Research (CUR; see page 97). With Brian Andreen's help, the ACS award for Research in Undergraduate Institutions funded by Research Corporation was introduced. They and the associations in which they were heavily involved were responsible for the programs that became AREA, REU, and RUI.

As I travel to liberal arts colleges these days I wonder if the faculty, or the institutions, realize just how much easier their research lives are because of those of us who worked so hard to change attitudes decades ago. It is easy to get the impression that college faculty are complacent. It is also taken, almost as a birthright, that research as it is practiced today will continue in these institutions.

Distractions

If undergraduate institutions aren't filling the nation's graduate schools, why does one need to spend money on undergraduate research in such places? Is it not far more economic, and better for the quality of research in American companies, for the graduate schools to recruit students in

75

Moscow and Beijing? To put it bluntly, *graduate programs in the sciences need the small colleges only as long as the small colleges produce good graduate students for their programs.* If the smaller colleges lose sight of that, or fail at it, review committees at the national level will notice quickly. Some already have.

Distractions are more abundant today on every campus. *When one walks through college science departments these days, one is treated to sociological experiments rather than organizations driven by undergraduate research, pre-professional education, and all of the things that made the American liberal arts college strong in the first place.* This is not to denigrate all of the causes of which Americans need be aware, but it behooves those in departments of chemistry to be chemists first—for without that, the justifications for their research become largely irrelevant.

In search of talent

I followed a practical path in developing the career that I have. When I took over as a department chair at Bowling Green in the early 1970s, it would have been easy to drop research and pursue an administrative career. I didn't do that. Now while I watch deans and presidents fall by the wayside when political whims at their institutions change, I'm glad I maintained my vigorous research presence and stayed in the faculty. At Hope, I chose a practical route as well. Research and instrumentation were necessary for faculty in smaller institutions to establish high esteem in the eyes of their peers. Looking back from a distance, I'd say that had we not done so, Hope specifically, and liberal arts colleges more generally, would be quite different places.

Liberal arts colleges of the current day have benefited from the arduous labors of many who went before. Responsibilities to the academy are more ominous these days than ever. A member of the advisory board of the Center for Photochemical Sciences put it this way. "My company," he said, "is a global company. By the year 2023 we anticipate that our research and development personnel will be spread around the world in a proportion almost parallel to the populations of their countries of origin." While in the early twentieth century, America became isolationist, closed its borders and kept the immigrants out, to do such a thing in the twenty-first century will only hurt us. As Bill Gates and Microsoft so successfully argued in their testimony before Congress, it is literally impossible for American industry to exist without tapping the intellectual skills of the world. And if we don't train the technically skilled in America,

American companies, now global enterprises, will move their research and development to foreign countries and find their skilled personnel elsewhere in the world.

We, in America, will have to fight hard in the years ahead just to maintain the strengths we have accumulated in the basic sciences. Enterprise in the world is changing so fast, that anticipating where to go next is becoming a real problem for our educational system. Some of the responsibility for keeping the American technical workforce strong lies with the liberal arts college. This much is certain. If colleges and universities don't serve the marketplace, the higher educational enterprise that is America's strongest calling card will decline in value in the early twenty-first century. Our enterprises will look elsewhere for talented people and for faculty that can teach them well. We'll have to work hard to avoid that, or the traditional pattern of undergraduate instruction in the sciences will pass from existence.

Some of the responsibility for keeping the American technical workforce strong lies with the liberal arts college.

The challenges of current-day research are more imposing and much more complex. America is a country of free enterprise, and the questions to the colleges will be the same continually put in front of all academicians as we face the future. Just what have you done for us lately? The question is in front of all of us right now. How we answer it will clearly determine what future we have in providing the pre-professional education of scientists. Æ

Acknowledgements: There are many, many students who made my stay at Hope College extraordinary. I appreciate them today as much as I did then. Pat Green edited this manuscript and read it on several occasions. Her help is gratefully acknowledged.

Like Doug Neckers, I am a product of a liberal arts institution. As a typical "premed" student at St. Mary's College in Winona, Minn., I wanted to go to medical school—mostly because I thought that was what one did with a biology major. Then Cal McNabb, at that time an assistant professor of biology, asked me if I would like to spend the summer doing a research project analyzing water on the upper Mississippi River. I was no fool: a summer of sunbathing, water skiing, and myriad other diversions lay ahead. I immediately said yes. How much work could there be?

Doing research as an undergraduate so captivated and excited me that it changed my mind about what could be done with a degree in biology. Here I was, a kid with some ability, little vision, Vietnam staring me in the face following graduation (it was 1968), and I learned something that no one else knew. I then told others about it by giving talks and publishing a paper! I not only wanted to pursue a research career, I wanted to do so in a manner that would help future students experience the joys of scientific investigation.

James M. Gentile is Dean of
Natural Sciences at Hope College.

JAMES M. GENTILE

6 THEN AND NOW: A BRIEF VIEW OF HOPE COLLEGE TODAY

JUST ENDING A SUCCESSFUL POSTDOCTORAL appointment at Yale, I was fortunate to have several job offers, but all were at research universities except the one from Hope College in Holland, Michigan. Hope was the only liberal arts college to which I applied. I knew nothing about the school, and even less about the church (Reformed Church in America) with which it was affiliated. Incredibly, I said yes to a job high in teaching hours, remarkably low in salary, unable to provide me with start-up funds, and with a conservative tradition and atmosphere that was 180 degrees from my liberal, Catholic background. Why? The answer was simple. Hope College reminded me of St. Mary's College in that the science faculty valued research as a necessary component of teaching, and the senior administrators with whom I talked during the interview process were all committed to achieving a successful integration of teaching and research at a small undergraduate institution.

Hope has grown since my arrival in 1976, and my role within the institution has changed. In my twenty-three years with the institution I have collaborated with well over 100 undergraduate students. I am now the dean for the Natural Science Division, and I still maintain an active research program in molecular mutagenesis that involves undergraduate students. It is important to note that the institution has gone out of it's way to make it possible for me to sustain my research while serving as dean.

Hope now has about 3000 students overall, with fifty-nine full-time-equivalent faculty in the seven departments that comprise science and mathematics. Though we have grown in numbers, we are still not considered a rich school, with an endowment of slightly over $100 million (small by the standards of other comparable liberal arts institutions). We are inordinately tuition-driven and not able to be as selective in enrollment as we would like. We have developed and sustained a strong science program because of the strength of tradition that has been handed down by faculty through the years from the early days of science at Hope. However, the bulk of the effort in programmatic planning to sustain our self-identified mission of integrating research and education, and to provide the energy and impetus to meet funding needs, is carried directly on the backs of science and mathematics faculty members. The Natural Science Division at Hope manages to run at a pace that is unique when compared to that of the institution at large; that and a science and mathematics faculty with *"fire in the belly"* for research with undergraduate students are the keys to our success.

Unfortunately, while faculty-student collaborative research is the sustaining hallmark of our program in science and mathematics, there is still only limited interest in integrating undergraduate students into research in programs outside of science and mathematics at Hope. It is important to note, however, that collaborations on curriculum innovations have increased between the science and mathematics faculty and colleagues from other divisions, and our hope is that such interactions may ultimately lead to other professional endeavors that do include students.

Research is teaching

The state of affairs today at Hope still rests on our belief that the underlying strength of our science and mathematics programs depends on the model that was developed in chemistry. Enhancing this model has been our ability to bridge the gaps between departments and work with students, and one another, at the interfaces of scientific disciplines. *We operate on the principle that undergraduate research is not only the essential component of good teaching and effective learning, but also that research with undergraduate students is in itself the purest form of teaching.* Therefore we recognize faculty who are actively engaged in academic-year research with students by counting that research into workload calculations.

We recognize faculty who are actively engaged in academic-year research with students by counting that research into workload calculations.

The collegial culture within the Division of Natural Sciences is the key ingredient in sustaining an intellectually vital learning community for faculty and students. Faculty and students work in a collaborative fashion, and upper-level students serve as mentors and role models for younger students in formal and informal capacities just as senior faculty mentor junior colleagues. Research collaborations are also prevalent among our faculty. Such collaborations allow us to adapt to the change in the research paradigm of the solitary researcher and provide logical interfaces of interest that stimulate excitement in the research laboratories, in the classrooms, and in the teaching laboratories. This helps to erode the feeling of intellectual isolation that frustrates faculty at many small institutions such as Hope.

Scholar-educators

Faculty are expected to be scholar-educators, and the administration is expected to sustain an infrastructure and environment to support student and faculty activities. The administration has worked hard and has been successful at meeting most infrastructure needs for our programs, and is now searching for funds to meet the critical need that we have for a new science facility. The faculty challenge one another to teach science and mathematics in an experiential mode that is steeped in investigation, from the introductory courses for all students through capstone experiences for all science and mathematics majors. While investigative, hands-on learning in class and laboratories is not research, it does provide students with many "tools of the trade" and begins to build in them a research-like thought process that helps them to learn science in a more intensive manner. We also have intentionally structured a curriculum in which students can extend the boundaries of departments to study at the interfaces of scientific disciplines. These curriculum goals stem from our commitment to scholarship for students and faculty alike, and we expect that students will be active learners who have a positive and productive experience in collaborative research.

Our faculty expect to become the best researchers and educators that they can be. Active scholarship promotes effective faculty and student learning, so scholarly activities must comprise an essential component for keeping our faculty vitally engaged. The definition of faculty scholarship at Hope includes pedagogical efforts as well as basic research, but

Faculty are expected to write research proposals and are rewarded for them, whether or not a grant results from that effort.

the fundamental tenets of scholarship as described in *Scholarship Assessed*[1] apply to all (see page 82). We recognize a variety of strengths within the Hope faculty, and, as is necessary for any healthy community, we strive to promote multiple ways through which faculty can develop individual and collective talents.

In the 1997 *Scholarship Assessed: Evaluation of the Professoriate,* the authors concluded that there is a common language in which to discuss the standards for scholarly work of all kinds:[2]

Clear goals
Are the basic purposes stated clearly? Are defined objectives realistic and achievable? Does the scholar identify important questions in the field?

Adequate preparation
Is the scholar conversant with the existing scholarship in the field? Does the scholar bring the necessary skills to the proposed work? Have the resources to move the project forward?

Appropriate methods
Are the scholar's methods appropriate to the goals? Are the methods applied effectively? Are the scholar's procedures modified for changing circumstances?

Significant results
Does the scholar achieve the goals? Does the work add consequentially to the field and open additional areas for further exploration?

Effective presentation
Is the work presented in a suitable style and organized effectively? Is the forum used appropriate to the intended audience? Is the message presented clearly?

Reflective critique
Is the work critically evaluated by the scholar? Does the scholar bring appropriate breadth to the critique? Does the scholar use the evaluation to improve the quality of future work?

Start-up funds are now routine in science and mathematics, with a range of $25,000 to upwards of $100,000 in some cases. In response to the institutional start-up commitment, faculty are expected to write research proposals and are rewarded for the writing and submission of proposals, whether or not a grant results from that effort. The success rate of proposals is very high, averaging about $900,000 in extramural funding for research and education programs in science and mathematics in each of the past seven years. About 60 percent of this new annual funding stems from proposals written to support overall program goals (e.g., NSF-Research Experiences for Undergraduates[REU] grants, Howard Hughes Medical Institute grants, Sherman Fairchild grants, etc.) and about an additional 25 percent of funding is for pedagogical efforts. I would like to see some increase in the number of basic research grant proposals that would more directly support faculty and student research. This is important because we have no endowment set aside to support student research. Summer student research stipends, and support of that research, is, wisely or not, too dependent on soft money.

Institutionally and divisionally, we work hard to help faculty to sustain professional excitement and productivity by providing over $150,000 annually for competitive faculty development awards. These resources are meant to provide research start-up leverage or to help fund research when a faculty member is in between funding periods. However, in recent years, some faculty have grown too dependent upon these internal resources, perhaps reducing the need (and desire) to go outside of the institution for larger sums of money. We are addressing this issue by trying to do a better job of tying internal support to innovative preliminary studies that bring researchers together for a specific research agenda and to requirements for the writing and submission of extramural, peer-reviewed proposals as a key outcome of the internal investment made by the institution.

A community of learners

An unusually high number of students (almost 40 percent) enter Hope with an interest in science and mathematics. During their days at Hope, we integrate students into a supportive community of learners that provides an environment rich in research-based learning opportunities. This past summer, 126 students did research with science and mathematics faculty, supported in part by five separate NSF-REU site awards (chemistry, biology, physics, computer science, mathematics). Many students indicate that the prospect of doing undergraduate research is a major deciding factor that helped them to identify Hope College as their choice for a college education. Although we do not have a research requirement, over 85 percent of Hope science and mathematics majors do research before they graduate. Approximately 30 percent of seniors graduate with a degree in science or mathematics. Of these, about 35 percent enter graduate school. According to a recent NSF study, our record in training students who achieve the Ph.D. is one of the strongest nationally. About 35 percent of our science and mathematics graduates seek to enter professional school. The ten-year acceptance rate for these students is 71 percent, and it is 90 percent for students who engage in research while at Hope.

Faculty members and students sustain vitality by engaging in research that has an impact in the professional communities.

Faculty members and students must sustain vitality by engaging in research that has an impact in the professional communities beyond the environment of Holland, Michigan.

83

NSF AWARDS FOR THE INTEGRATION OF RESEARCH AND EDUCATION

"Research and education are two sides of the same coin: Discovery," read a 1998 NSF press release announcing the recipients of their Awards for the Integration of Research and Education (AIRE).[3] The awards were made to ten undergraduate institutions selected for finding innovative ways to integrate their education and research activities. "These . . . awards help create a discovery-rich environment where institutions and their students can benefit by making research an essential component of the college curricula," said the NSF.

AIRE recipients received $500,000 over three years to design and implement programs that extend initiatives they had already undertaken to integrate research and education. The institutions are expected to provide undergraduates with experiences rooted in the process of discovery and to set the stage for students' life-long inquiry and learning.

Hope College was among the ten awardees. Their AIRE is funding: a visiting scholars program in which senior faculty from other institutions work with Hope faculty on research projects and their integration into new courses at both Hope and the visiting scholar's home institution; small grants to encourage faculty to integrate their own research into classes throughout the curriculum; summer research scholarships for K–12 education students; and summer workshops to help high school teachers incorporate research-based teaching into their classes.

Hope College faculty rank fourth of all liberal arts institutions for numbers of faculty research publications and fourteenth overall for highest impact of those publications as measured by the Science Citation Index.[4,5] We must be a bit guarded in our interpretation of these numbers, however. As with any institution, the publication rates of faculty members in any given department vary considerably (indeed there are some departments in which one or two faculty members are responsible for the majority of publications on an annual basis) and the impact of publications for an institution or department may result from only a few, very highly received papers. Nevertheless, the publication value-added of the science currently produced at Hope College is significant. Since 1990 over 350 undergraduate students have coauthored research publications with science and mathematics faculty. Corporate and university recruiters have identified the value-added component of experience in research and teaching laboratories as the key attribute that students carry with them beyond Hope. Research in and out of class promotes in students critical thinking, reasoning and problem-solving traits that are essential to success in any endeavor.

PROJECT KALEIDOSCOPE

Project Kaleidoscope (PKAL) is an informal national alliance of individuals, institutions and organizations committed to strengthening undergraduate science, mathematics, engineering, and technology education. Since its beginning in 1989, PKAL has been shaped by two goals: To transform the learning environment for undergraduate students by building institutional teams with a driving vision of *what works* and a commitment to action; and to foster public understanding of how a strong undergraduate science community serves the national interest.

PKAL's *What Works* recognizes that the most important attribute of undergraduate programs that attract and sustain student interest is a thriving natural science community where students:
- engage in learning that is experiential and steeped in investigation from general introductory courses to capstone courses for science majors;
- engage in learning that makes critical connections between the classroom, lab, different disciplines, the undergraduate and educational community, the nation, and the world;
- come together with faculty as partners in learning in a setting where faculty are as committed to undergraduate teaching as they are to their own intellectual vitality.

"What works is where there is strong institutional support to build and sustain such communities of learners."[6]

The current program at Hope continues to take its lead from the sustaining tradition of excellence that has infused chemistry at Hope since the days of the pioneering chemist researcher-educators, Gerrit Van Zyl and Harvey Kleinheksel. Building upon this tradition, all of the departments in the natural sciences have grown in stature, resulting in recognition by Project Kaleidoscope with an award as a "Whole Program that Works" (above) and by the NSF with an Award for the Integration of Research and Education (page 84).

Can we do better? Sure, who couldn't? Have we made mistakes? Yes, who hasn't? But are we an example of what can be done at a small institution with a commitment shared by faculty and administration? I answer with a resounding yes! We have built upon the achievements of a long tradition of faculty and administrators who have given Hope their best. For all that I am thankful. Æ

A SMALL, TRADITIONAL LIBERAL ARTS college like Hendrix must be concerned to preserve and enhance its central values: to endow the student with capacities for learning, not simply to inculcate facts; to encourage dispositions of curiosity and inquiry, rather than to teach rote knowledge; and to instill a sense of intellectual leadership, so that our students understand that they can be the peers of any undergraduates, anywhere.

As dean, my function is to enable the faculty to do their work and do it better. I strive constantly to remind them that it is their work, not mine, that is the core of the college. Tangible and material support must follow in the form of departmental budgets, equipment and supplies, sabbaticals, reasonable teaching loads, opportunities for professional development and research.

John Churchill is Vice President for Academic Affairs
and Dean of Hendrix College.

John Churchill

7 MENTORS IN SCIENCE: RESEARCH-BASED PEDAGOGY AT HENDRIX COLLEGE

THE PATH TOWARD EXCELLENCE in undergraduate science instruction at Hendrix College began amid one of the great cultural controversies of the twentieth century. In 1928, following the Scopes "Monkey" Trial in neighboring Tennessee, the people of Arkansas enacted an initiated referendum—a direct popular ballot measure—that forbade the teaching of evolution in the state's public schools, colleges, and universities. The response of Hendrix College, an independent Methodist-related institution led by President John Hugh Reynolds, was to raise $300,000—half from the General Education Board of New York (the forerunner of the Rockefeller Foundation) and half from the municipal utility corporation in its hometown of Conway, Arkansas—to construct a building in which science could be taught without political intervention. That structure, eventually named Reynolds Hall, still shelters the teaching of science. In 1998–1999 a reconstruction and renovation began, which nearly tripled its original size, and provided facilities for the twenty-first century. In the same school year, an entirely new building for housing scientific instruction rose two hundred yards away. In the 1920s Hendrix faced down the political opponents of science; at the beginning of a new century, Hendrix is constructing buildings to facilitate a new day in undergraduate science instruction.

What has that new day brought? Science pedagogy at the close of the twentieth century has developed into a set of sophisticated strategies to educate the scientists, health care professionals, teachers, and professors of the future. We now know that becoming a scientist, or a professional in a science-based discipline, depends critically on induction into a community of scientific practice: a group of teaching and learning researchers—faculty and students together—whose relation to their discipline is not limited to the transmission and absorption of established knowledge. That relation, rather, is oriented by the purpose of *turning students into practicing scientists in their disciplines*. This aim is more complex and more interesting than simply passing on facts. It involves developing in students the habits of mind that enable them to see situations and conceive problems as chemists and physicists see and conceive them. It involves developing in students the capacities of hypothesis forma-

Hendrix's "in-house champion" of the vision of research-based teaching, Thomas Goodwin, guides a student through a chemistry experiment.

tion, experimental design, and technical skill to practice the scientific method. It involves developing in students the ability to take and construe data, to present results, and to draw conclusions. Developing these capacities is not, fundamentally, a matter of coming to command facts, but of induction into the practice of science. How are such teaching and learning communities developed?

Ingredients for success

The first essential ingredient is direct professional contact between research-active faculty and students. Faculty must not only be accessible to students, they must see students as more than receptacles for the input of knowledge. They must provide entreé for students into the world of scientific practice. Faculty in such a community should see students as prospective collaborators. Their interest in students must be a positive mentoring relationship, in which students' conceptions of themselves as budding researchers come to be

The first essential ingredient at Hendrix is direct professional contact between research-active faculty and students.

modeled on the mentor's example. This sort of relationship requires not only effective guidance, but demands that the faculty member be engaged in meaningful research—work that is assessed by external peer review through the grant-seeking process and through the evaluation of results for publication. *External review validates the faculty member's work.* Publications lend strength to grant applications, grants fuel research, and research enables publication. This cycle grounds the faculty member's work in the standards of a scientific discipline, and ensures that the local community of scientific practice into which the student researcher is inducted is a functioning element of the validated and validating networks of that discipline.

Perhaps the most important feature of this model of science pedagogy is its denial of familiar, false dichotomies. The conventional wisdom is that research and teaching are competitive, mutually inhibiting pursuits, and that academic science divides into research institutions and teaching institutions (see *Scholarship Reconsidered,* page 63). But, if some of the most important teaching consists of involvement in research, then we need faculty and institutions who see research and teaching not as competitive—or even complementary—but as blended. It is important to see that this perspective is not merely the claim that teaching and research enhance each other. It is the claim that research, done in the right way, in the right institutional context, can be the most effective instruction. We are describing not a symbiosis but a synthesis.

How can such a vision become institutionalized? First, a college needs an in-house champion of this vision. Hendrix had—and has—Tom Goodwin. Mentored in a small-college, undergraduate chemistry department, Goodwin came to Hendrix in the late 1970s with a vision of this synthesis and a passion to make it possible on this campus. He led by example, conducting research with undergraduates under adverse conditions most charitably described as benign neglect. He secured grants through sheer dint of hard work, opportunistic networking, and qualities of moxie, gall, and chutzpah. When he needed to push, he pushed. When pleading was needed, he pleaded. When vision was called for, he inspired. When he needed to drag the dean and president out for pizza with his students, he did that. The vision and the hard work centered on one

In 1979 Thomas Goodwin received a grant from Research Corporation for what he had described as "Maytansinoid Synthesis." This was one of the hottest synthetic targets in the field at that time, and many of the leading research groups at major universities were engaged in their synthesis. Was it sheer arrogance or creative genius that compelled Goodwin to make this proposal? The community paid attention.

> *Ever since the launching of Sputnik thirty-five years ago, Americans have been obsessed with science education reform. Task forces meet and commissions recommend, but little makes its way from the edge to the center of the educational process. What is new and different—New Math, or self-paced instruction, or writing across the curriculum, or teacher competence—is initally embraced, but hard to locate only a few years later. In education there appears to be a strong default mechanism, inertia in the system, that educational reform, as currently practiced, rarely diverts or modifies.*
>
> —Revitalizing Undergraduate Science, *Sheila Tobias, 1992*[1]

thing: achieving a seamless integration of the faculty member's identity as a researching scientist and teacher. Any college proposing to enter this pedagogy needs a champion like Tom Goodwin.

It also needs a character like Warfield Teague—a quartermaster general, a planning and logistics champion—who can take a vision from conception to implementation. Himself research-active, Teague was, and is, the guiding force at Hendrix who has led the facilities design process resulting in 120,000 square feet of new labs, teaching, and office space in one planning and construction effort.

But perhaps the most essential function of these senior faculty has been their recruitment of junior members who share the vision and the energy necessary to make it real. The three members of the Hendrix chemistry department who have joined the staff since Goodwin's arrival have entered fully into the synthesis of research and teaching. They are securing grants, conducting research with undergraduates, and publishing the results.

The most essential function of senior faculty has been their recruitment of junior members who share the vision and the energy necessary to make it real.

The next ingredient is bright, capable students, who have the desire not just to learn scientific facts but to participate in the processes that establish facts and test theories. These students need more than curiosity; they need the self-discipline and capacity for hard work that will make them flourish in the laboratory. Hendrix has attracted such students in large measure because of a strong regional reputation for premedical education. However an institution initially attracts such students, it will induct them into a community of scientific practice—as defined above—only through the activities of the faculty.

Central values

In all of this, a small, traditional liberal arts college like Hendrix must be concerned to preserve and enhance its central values: to endow the students with capacities for learning, not simply to inculcate facts; to encourage dispositions of curiosity and inquiry, rather than to teach rote knowledge; and to instill a sense of intellectual leadership, so that our students understand that they can be the peers of any undergraduates, anywhere. The evidence is strong that Hendrix has been successful in this objective. Our annual student delegation to the meetings of the American Chemical Society includes an average of fourteen who make presentations. An annual average of five student physicists present papers at the American Physical Society meetings or at the National Conferences on Undergraduate Research (NCUR; see page 52). NCUR attracted thirty-nine Hendrix presentations in all disciplines in 1998, and forty-four in 1999. These delegations are among the largest at NCUR in absolute numbers, and also when considered as a proportion of total institutional enrollment. Hendrix students also make presentations annually at state and regional symposia in philosophy, psychology, sociology, and other disciplines.

The learning communities which make this success possible themselves require careful nurture. This support requires a combination of several components.

Faculty and students alike must be made mindful of the institutional value placed on undergraduate research. An important way to accomplish this aim is to talk about it. At Hendrix, the president, the academic officers and faculty who make presentations to prospective or incoming students all make certain that their audiences understand this institutional priority.

Departmental budgets must reflect the cost of this instructional format. Specifically, supply budgets will likely need enhancement, and the institution must be ready to do whatever it takes to encourage students to travel to national meetings to present research results.

Researchers must be provided with equipment. At Hendrix, year by year, we have found the means and the will to equip laboratories for undergraduate investigation. Grant proposals to the National Science Foundation and to private foundations are written and supported by the institution. Funding priorities are arranged to match the grants.

Faculty work patterns must change and the changes need institutional endorsement. Institutional expectations of faculty in teaching load, and of departments in course offerings, will need adjustment to reflect the realities of the time and energy devoted to the supervision of research. At Hendrix the departments of physics and chemistry, in preparing a proposal to Research Corporation for a Department Development Award, gained administrative approval for teaching loads that explicitly recognized the direction of undergraduate research—four course equivalents per year. Sabbaticals and leaves had to be available to help faculty gain and retain needed expertise. Hendrix adopted an accelerated sabbatical schedule for physicists and chemists under the Research Corporation grant. Departing from standard rotations, in 1994 Hendrix placed physics and chemistry on an immediate one-sabbatical-per-year schedule. The administration of the college proactively insisted that sabbaticals be not merely available but used to maximum advantage by faculty members. Sabbatical activities were negotiated to increase the likelihood that students would benefit directly from the faculty member's project. Hendrix must be ready to form partnerships with corporations and foundations in support of faculty projects that may begin in sabbaticals and continue thereafter.

Facilities—buildings and equipment—must be provided, often by arranging the institution's most fundamental priorities toward the provision of adequate classrooms, offices, and laboratories. Hendrix began planning new science facilities—sorely needed ones—in the late 1980s. By 1999, 100,000 square feet of new laboratory, classroom, and office space was under construction, and another 20,000 was under renovation. And not only must the buildings be provided, they must be designed for this pedagogy (see page 94). Every member of the five affected departments at Hendrix participated in the design process for these buildings, sitting for hours with the architects and with Research Facilities

---

Science education in liberal arts colleges thrives best in an atmosphere that is saturated with opportunities for undergraduate research. Students in such programs engage science through apprenticeship education; faculty maintain active professional lives that support both research and teaching; and the department develops a vigorous mission shared by faculty and students that serves goals of both science and education.

—What Works: Building Natural Science Communities,
Project Kaleidoscope, 1991[2]

Design of San Diego, explaining pedagogy, functional relationships, and design needs. Senior chemist Warfield Teague coordinated this process. Office and laboratory proximity have to accord with the demands of research supervision. Offices themselves have to be designed as teaching spaces.

Therefore, the new Hendrix facilities have faculty offices of about 180–200 square feet, affording the usual amenities as well as a seminar table for instructional use within the office. Ample public spaces for students to study in, to converse with each other in, and to use for informal interactions with faculty, are important parts of such buildings. Much important learning takes places in hallways, lounges, write-up rooms, and other less-formally designed spaces. Communities need such public spaces in which to interact. And of course, labs not only for regular courses, but also for undergraduate research, are essential.

Staffing, both faculty and laboratory technical support staff, must be adequate to the new patterns of work. With assistance from Research Corporation, Hendrix added one new faculty member in chemistry and one in physics, as well as full-time technical support personnel in both departments. The college independently added similar positions in other science disciplines. Hendrix made all these commitments, adding new faculty positions, adding technical support staff, augmenting budgets, and placing institutional priority on the construction and renovation of the aforementioned science facilities.

Leadership

How did all this come to be a reality at Hendrix? I have already mentioned the ingredients: human, in the faculty and students, and material, in the budgets and buildings. The ingredients combined into the reality because of a shared vision and shared persistence. President Ann H. Die came to Hendrix in 1992 with strong support for the faculty's focus on the excellence of the academic program. She encouraged faculty initiatives to build centers of strength while elevating across the board an already superb program. The *Leadership in a small college* most visible faculty initiative has been, *must have multiple dimensions.* of course, the undergraduate research program in the sciences. President Die's support has come through three central characteristics. First, she has responded to opportunity. She recognized a project in the sciences with tremendous potential and embraced it. She saw the opportunity to build upon a historic institutional

FACILITIES: SUPPORTING A COMMUNITY

It is clear that a highly interactive, hands-on, experiential, lab-rich, problem-solving program for natural science communities places special demands on infrastructure. Facilities, equipment, computing, libraries, and technical support must be adequate to the job if we are to achieve the fundamental reform of science and mathematics education needed by this country. . . .

Architecture and facilities must support good teaching and learning. . . . We have come to recognize a widespread mismatch on most campuses between the pedagogy supported by the existing facilities and the pedagogy we seek to encourage. Why this mismatch between architecture and curriculum? In part, because architects are often unfamiliar with the approach to undergraduate science and mathematics education. . . . Faculty, furthermore, have few models of building design which translate these functions into form.

A program of undergraduate science and mathematics education that seeks to attract students rather than weed them out needs spaces organized differently from the kinds of spaces built in the 1950s and 1960s. These earlier spaces, with large lecture halls and relatively cramped laboratories envisioned a science education characterized by passive rather than active learning. Ironically, just as experimental research in science became more collaborative, our methods of teaching science became less so.

—*What Works: Building Natural Science Communities,*
Project Kaleidoscope, 1991[3]

Completed in fall 2000, John Hugh Reynolds Hall is part of The Charles D. Morgan Center for Physical Sciences at Hendrix College.

> *Research and scholarship are a matter of vision, persistent and able faculty, a little money, and an administration that value them. Science is dead in the classroom without the quickening spirit of investigation.*
>
> —What Works: Building Natural Science Communities,
> Project Kaleidoscope, 1991 [4]

strength. Science pedagogy, undergraduate research, and the buildings projects surged to the top of the priority list because the president saw the prospect of dramatic advance. Second, she has been persistent in fund-raising. She committed herself and the college's fund-raising capacities to the task of finding over $24 million in construction funding, and she has accomplished it. Another dimension of persistence accounts for President Die's third characteristic—constancy of vision. Any human undertaking with multiple participants undergoes phases in which enthusiasm, understanding of purpose, and degree of commitment wax and wane among the individuals and groups involved. So has it been at Hendrix in the advancement of undergraduate research. A department unified in its commitment to accelerated sabbaticals will begin to come unstuck when it comes down to a certain faculty member actually being willing to uproot his or her life for a year. A department eager to embrace research expectations will quail a bit in assessing a junior member for tenure. In cases like these, administrative persistence in vision is essential. At Hendrix this initiative for undergraduate research came from faculty. But once the college embraced it administratively, the president has held everyone's feet to the fire. Without that, we would certainly have failed.

But leadership in a small college must have multiple dimensions. Top-down, directive presidential leadership cannot create a thriving science program without faculty vision and energy. Even a visionary leader cannot inspire faculty to efforts that must be driven primarily by love of the discipline, love of students, and love of teaching. On the other hand, faculty vision and energy are wasted without enthusiasm at the senior administrative level, since no faculty, no matter how capable, can raise its own building funds and redirect institutional priorities. The coordination of administrative leadership and faculty initiative requires careful work by the college's academic officers—deans and area (or division) chairs. At Hendrix all three levels of administration and execution have worked with remarkable persistence, skill, and commonality of vision.

To these ingredients must be added the dimension of national networking. Our faculty are in contact with the important national developments. Again, opportunism, vision, and persistence are essential. As stated above, an important feature of the advance at Hendrix was the work of Tom Goodwin, our quintessential fire-in-the-belly man. It was Goodwin who cultivated ties to Research Corporation and to the Dreyfus Foundation. Goodwin networked at the Gordon Research Conferences and with the Council on Undergraduate Research (see page 97). A background of networking—including Goodwin's year as president of the Council on Undergraduate Research in 1992–1993—made the name Hendrix College a familiar one in advantageous places. The difference between being unknown and being known came through the persistence of an individual who seized opportunities to make and maintain contacts in national organizations.

Above all, however, we have had the advantage of being in a context of robust institutional health and growing collegiate prestige and recognition. The advent of research-based instruction at Hendrix has both benefited from and contributed to that institutional advance.

Investment

What investment was required? The college has been adding new faculty positions at the rate of about one or two per year over the last decade and a half. Higher shares of these new positions have gone to research-active departments. Biology has received two new positions in that time period, psychology two, sociology and anthropology one, philosophy one, and mathematics and computer science two. In two cases, chemistry and physics, additions to the departments—both in faculty and in technical support staff—have been tied explicitly to a partnership forged between Hendrix and Research Corporation of Tucson, Arizona, a partnership whose purpose was the enhancement of undergraduate research. Chemistry went from three faculty in 1980 to five in 1999. Physics went from two to four. The college independently added faculty, technical support, and clerical support, to other departments as well. There is no doubt that the Research Corporation investment in Hendrix—$588,000 over five years—made possible advances that would otherwise not have occurred. And there is also no doubt that the Research Corporation inspiration, properly adapted to local circumstances, has motivated other departments as well. The college is now on the brink of an analogous partnership which will enhance our program in

THE COUNCIL ON UNDERGRADUATE RESEARCH

The Council on Undergraduate Research (CUR) marks its beginning from the 1978 publication of *Research in Chemistry at Private Undergraduate Colleges,* by Brian Andreen, a directory that descibed work in progress by college faculty and background data on each department (originally 93, the 1999 directory lists 558 departments). In hopes of addressing the disparity in recognition of research between graduate and undergraduate chemistry departments, Andreen also organized a representative team of ten college faculty to form the initial council and assist him in the development of CUR's first directory. In 1979, nine of the ten "councilors" met in Pittsburgh to determine if CUR should continue and in what form. Their enthusiastic decision was to formalize the organization and to initiate continuing efforts such as the *CUR Newsletter,* conferences, and regular editions of the directory.[5]

In its first four years CUR focused only on chemistry departments in private liberal arts colleges. Today, there are divisions of biology, engineering, geology, math and computer science, physics and astronomy, and psychology, and all primarily undergraduate institutions are included. The scope of its programs and projects has expanded as well:

• **Summer Undergraduate Fellowships** are awarded to students interested in pursuing their research interests at primarily undergraduate institutions. The fellowships provide an opportunity for students and faculty mentors to engage in approximately ten weeks of full-time research.

• **CUR Fellows Awards** regognize deserving faculty and undergraduate research.

• **Undergraduate Research Posters on Capitol Hill** is an event that occurs annually in April. Sixty competitively-selected student posters are displayed at the U.S. Capitol during an afternoon reception.

• **The Institutional Liaison Service** at campuses throughout the country helps spread the word about CUR and its programs. The **Consulting-Mentoring Service** offers assistance to undergraduate mathematics and engineering departments, divisions, or faculty members. The **Speaker's Bureau** provides an opportunity for institutions to host visiting lecturers who share first-hand experience about high-caliber science being conducted in undergraduate programs.

• **Research Link 2000** is a project to bring together biology faculty to select, develop and disseminate experimental systems and instructional materials to support research-based experiments in introductory biology courses.

• **Materials Research** promotes collaboration between faculty and NSF Materials Research Centers or other faculty who already have NSF support.

mathematics and computer science, augmenting its technical dimension while assuring its theoretical depth and its liberal arts orientation.

I have alluded above to the need for buildings to house classrooms, offices, laboratories, and the critical public spaces in which learning communities take shape. Hendrix's burgeoning programs in science until 1999–2000 have been housed in buildings reflecting the institutional scale and pedagogical styles of the middle 1960s. Now nearing completion are projects totaling $24,000,000 for new and completely rebuilt space for biology, chemistry, mathematics and computer science, physics, and psychology. In order to make these projects happen, it was necessary to focus the institution's priorities—its planning efforts, its fundraising, its on- and off-campus constituencies' senses of purpose—on this effort. To focus the institution's priorities means to secure the support of multiple constituencies. At the foundation, academic priorities must flow from the faculty and the academic administration. Every college has planning processes, planning documents, strategic consultations among faculty and deans. At Hendrix the project of focusing institutional priorities began there. Administrative support is essential, and then—critically—support from the Board of Trustees. Faculty vision will remain vision only until trustees provide and find the means to realize them. Hendrix students and faculty are occupying new science buildings every fall from 1999 through 2000 to 2001.

How can this excellence be maintained? The old saw that success breeds success is true in this sense: excellence is an acquired habit, and once an institution establishes its benchmarks, a tradition of superb performance can become habitual. Hendrix exchanged old benchmarks, based on local and traditional criteria of excellence, for new ones based on national and contemporary criteria. How are these criteria developed? The answer lies in the networking discussed above. Hendrix personnel talked to the best people at the best places, and framed their vision accordingly. But habits are sustained by activity, and the maintenance, even enhancement, of a tradition of excellence requires constant vigilance. Faculty need support, encouragement, nurturing. Presidents and deans should tell them every day that their work is the college's reason for existence. Tangible and material support must follow in the form of departmental budgets, equipment and supplies, sabbaticals, reasonable teaching loads, opportunities for professional development and research.

Success breeds success: excellence is an acquired habit.

The maintenance of the conditions of excellence in research-based pedagogy is surely possible in an institution of any size or character. But small liberal arts colleges are uniquely equipped to facilitate those conditions. Communities of small scale, in which faculty and students know each other, in which learning groups form readily, and in which research opportunities are widely available to students so that they become the norm rather than the exception, are by nature most suited for the development and implementation of this style of instruction and inquiry. Nothing about being a small liberal arts college guarantees this outcome, but the institutional character provides a head start, a head start we have exploited at Hendrix with great success. Æ

THE FACULTY AT FURMAN HAVE held steadfastly to the fundamental beliefs that undergraduate research (joint faculty-student research) of publishable quality is not only compatible with chemical education, but is actually vital to its effectiveness; that first-rate instrumental and laboratory facilities are essential to the practice of modern chemistry and critical in eliciting excitement among students and faculty alike; that a commitment to excellence in both teaching and professional activities are key individual goals; and that financial resourcefulness and independence are crucial to developing a first-rate chemistry program.

Larry S. Trzupek (left) and Lon B. Knight, Jr. are Professors of Chemistry at Furman University.

Larry S. Trzupek and Lon B. Knight, Jr.

8 CHEMICAL BONDING BETWEEN STUDENTS AND FACULTY AT FURMAN UNIVERSITY

Furman University is a private, liberal arts college of 2,640 undergraduate students located in Greenville, South Carolina. Nationally ranked (Carnegie Liberal Arts I), Furman attracts talented students from almost every state and several foreign countries: the average SAT score of the most recent freshman class was 1250, over 10 percent were valedictorians or salutatorians, and 59 percent were ranked in the top 10 percent of their high school graduating class. Since its founding in 1826 and continuing until 1992, Furman was governed by the State Baptist Convention of South Carolina. In 1992, the Convention severed its relationship with the university, and Furman became an independent college governed by a self-perpetuating board of trustees. Furman moved to a new 750-acre campus site located seven miles north of downtown Greenville in the late 1950s. Over the past eight years, the university has initiated $83 million in new construction; its endowment is approximately $220 million.

With nine faculty, the chemistry department offers the American Chemical Society B.S. degree in chemistry which includes the biochemistry and environmental certifications (page 122). It also operates a research-oriented master's program designed primarily as a fifth year of study for Furman's own students. The university funds the M.S. program, which averages about seven students per year, through assistantships and tuition waivers.

The centerpiece of the chemistry curriculum is a summer undergraduate research program which is one of the largest in the nation. Chemistry's undergraduate research emphasis has served as a model program for the university, which supports and encourages such activities in all academic disciplines under its strategic initiative of "engaged learning." Furman's current and tenth president, Dr. David E. Shi, is an enthusiastic supporter of the university's effort to increase engaged learning opportunities for all students.

The chemistry program: Origin and mission

The chemistry program's emphasis on undergraduate research began in the early 1960s with a summer research program that consisted of two

Furman University Chemistry Department Faculty, Bottom row, from left: Charles A. Arrington, Timothy W. Hanks, Noel P. Kane-Maguire, Lon B. Knight, Jr., Moses N.F. Lee. Top row, from left: Larry S. Trzupek, Jeffrey T. Petty, John F. Wheeler, Sandra K. Wheeler, Laura L. Wright.

students and a comparable number of faculty. Over the next four decades that number has steadily grown, reaching a level of eleven to twelve faculty (including visiting professors from nearby institutions) and nearly fifty undergraduate participants; over the past eight years, the number of postdoctoral research associates has grown from one to five with the help of external grants and internal departmental funding. As substantiated by a number of quantifiable measures (data presented in later sections), the program has achieved a national reputation for excellence in undergraduate education. Each year since 1991, Furman's program has ranked among the top four undergraduate institutions in the number of ACS-certified B.S. degrees awarded in chemistry, according to annual data published in *Chemical and Engineering News*; for the past several years our rank in this category has been in the top twenty-five among all types of institutions.

The faculty have held steadfastly to the fundamental beliefs that undergraduate research (joint faculty-student research) of publishable quality is not only compatible with chemical education, but is actually vital to its effectiveness; that first-rate instrumental and laboratory facilities are essential to the practice of modern chemistry and critical in eliciting excitement among students and faculty alike; that a commitment to excellence in both teaching and professional activities are key individual goals; that financial resourcefulness and independence are crucial to developing a first-rate chemistry program; that selection and hiring of new faculty and vigorous recruiting of potential students are key to establishing the "chemistry" necessary for a successful department; and that the establishment of a rigorous yet flexible curriculum is needed to allow efficient updating without having to reinvent its foundation.

The fundamental factor in establishing the basis for the current success of the department was the absolute commitment of the early faculty—led by Stuart Patterson (Furman tenure, 1954–1988) and Don Kubler (1961–1985)—to the concept of undergraduate research as an essential component of every chemistry major's college experience. Their thinking was profoundly influenced by the intense and productive interactions that John R. Sampey (1934–1964) had with students during his Furman career. Another influence was the highly successful National Science Foundation-sponsored Institute for High School Teachers (1959–1962) directed by Albert Southern, whose longtime service to Furman (1934–1947 and 1958–1973) has been recognized by an endowed lectureship. One of Professor Southern's physical chemistry students at Furman in the late 1930s was Charles H. Townes, who received the Nobel Prize in physics in 1964 for pioneering work in the development of the maser and laser.

The fundamental factor in establishing the basis for the current success of the department was the absolute commitment of the early faculty.

With the introduction of a new chemistry curriculum in the 1960s, independent study—which in all but very rare cases meant participation in an undergraduate research project with thesis—became a graduation requirement for all chemistry majors. Not only would students master laboratory skills, learn to analyze and interpret new data, and gain creative thinking experience, but more importantly, they would witness on a daily basis and jointly participate in the passion for scientific investigation as actually practiced by their faculty mentors. Undergraduate research in this setting was not intended to focus on the repetition of complex and difficult exercises with known outcomes. The chemistry program was founded on the excitement associated with a journey into the unknown, and it is the continued pursuit of this dimension that has sustained and guided our program. (We have more unknown now than

ever!) Faculty hiring and retention, student recruitment, space allocation, curriculum development, library holdings, equipment acquisitions,
departmental fund raising and budget de-

The chemistry program was founded on the excitement associated with a journey into the unknown.

cisions, and corporate interactions are all
designed and managed with a single objective: *to create an environment in which
each faculty member, working closely with
students, can become a nationally-recognized and respected scientist in his or
her field of chemistry.*

This "grand experiment," begun in the early 1960s and conducted in
the small-college setting, has proven to be a most effective educational
model for undergraduate chemistry students and their faculty mentors.
The department's success stems from the ability of this research focus to
sustain faculty excitement in and commitment to their academic discipline. All other programmatic components are derived from this single
objective. Our vision for the future is the same: overcome every obstacle
and take advantage of every opportunity which presents itself so that
each faculty member can be recognized and respected as an accomplished
scientist and as a researcher who works with students in a passionate
and dedicated manner. This well-established consistency of purpose has
proven to be a dynamic, exciting and successful strategy for the operation of an undergraduate chemistry program in the setting of a liberal
arts college. Problem-solving skills acquired by students engaged in research constitute a key feature of their education, and dedication to and
support for this effort represents a most noble commitment of time and
resources.

The focus of the curriculum: Research with undergraduates

It is important to emphasize the deliberate efforts that are made to
tailor specific aspects of the chemistry curriculum in support of the departmental philosophy towards undergraduate research. Many of the features of the program are designed to prepare majors for the summer research experience by integrating the material found in traditional courses.
The integrated "Techniques" laboratory features student adaptation of
procedures found in the chemical literature, utilization of sequences of
reactions in preparative procedures, and the application of contemporary techniques for compound identification and purification. All of these
features provide valuable preparation for student independence in the
research environment. Indeed, completion of the "Techniques" labora-

tory, a sophomore level course, is the usual prerequisite for participation in the summer research program. Finally, since most student researchers will participate in manuscript preparation and presentation of their work at a professional meeting, the background they receive in searching the literature, speaking in seminar and carrying out technical writing assignments in their preparatory course work will directly facilitate these professional opportunities.

In introductory courses, faculty regularly and consciously mention student or faculty research in connection with topics covered in the course, and in so doing, begin to communicate both the relevance and excitement of such work. In this way, beginning with their initial chemistry courses, students are aware that scientific research does occur in the department and realize that in one or two years they may be participating in that research. In the very first lecture of Chemistry 11, the different areas of chemistry are presented by showing a photograph of the faculty and identifying each person by area of chemistry and the type of research being conducted. These references to research occur in many instances throughout the undergraduate curriculum.

While the department pursues a number of educational goals, its emphasis on undergraduate research provides a focus for the program. No matter what a major's ultimate career goal—a B.S.- level technical position, medical school, law school, a position in business or industry, graduate study in chemistry—the department believes that the problem-solving abilities developed in pursuing a genuine research project are of inestimable value in every student's educational experience. Similarly, *the department sets forth as an ideal for its faculty national recognition in their area of specialization.* That recognition can take a variety of forms. Examples include Lon Knight's selection to chair a Gordon Research Conference, John Wheeler's invitation to compile a review on contemporary applications of capillary electrophoresis and Moses Lee's invitation to participate in the Annual National Science Foundation Workshop on Organic Synthesis and Natural Products Chemistry. These philosophical commitments to undergraduate research center on the development of chemistry majors as independent scientists capable of clear and organized thought, and it is in this context that the department has been able to build within the university administration a solid and consistent

While the department pursues a number of educational goals, its emphasis on undergraduate research provides a focus for the program.

base of support for this approach to liberal undergraduate education.

All of our undergraduate research activities are managed as a cohesive and cooperative departmental program as opposed to the simple sum of individual efforts. Eligible students are required to attend all faculty research presentations in early spring of each year. The active "recruitment" of students by individual faculty members is discouraged since we believe it is most important for students to be aware of all the available research areas before they make a final choice. Following these faculty presentations, the students make formal applications to the summer research program and indicate, in order of preference, their top three choices of research directors. The department chair then conducts private conversations with students in order to achieve a healthy balance between student choices for research directors and the number of students each faculty member can accommodate in a given year.

We believe that this departmental perspective also contributes to the success of the chemistry research program by fostering collaborative interactions between the "faculty" groups. In a relatively small department, such interactions not only provide an important added faculty stimulus, but also considerably broaden student experiences via joint group meetings and team participation. At present, the majority of the faculty have at least one collaborative research project involving one or more other faculty members. For example, Drs. Knight and Arrington have an extensive joint publication record, where advantage is taken of their respective experimental and computational strengths. Likewise, Drs. Wright and Petty are involved in a joint biochemical project whose success is dependent on their respective expertise with atomic force microscopy and scanning tunneling microscopy (AFM/STM) instrumentation and biophysical chemistry. A similar cooperative effort between the research groups of Drs. Hanks and Wright is being actively pursued in the conducting polymer and nanotechnology areas. These collaborative efforts extend to grant submissions to external funding agencies, as evidenced in the current joint Research Corporation Cottrell College Science Award of Drs. Wheeler and Kane-Maguire to study selective binding of chiral metal complexes using capillary electrophoresis.

Undergraduate research presents a different type of learning opportu-

Collaborative interactions between the faculty groups not only provide an important faculty stimulus, but broaden student experiences via joint group meetings and team participation.

nity (compared to conventional courses that operate in the setting of limited time and contact) for students to develop and display talents that are quite distinct from those that are required to make high grades in traditional science courses. The key ingredients for research achievement include interest, enthusiasm, tenacity and a strong work ethic. In fact, it is not uncommon to find an inverse correlation between GPAs and laboratory research potential. The growth and self-confidence acquired by these "weaker" students through the

The key ingredients for research achievement include interest, enthusiasm, tenacity and a strong work ethic.

student-faculty research experience is truly an inspirational "high" for the faculty. We remember well the struggling "C" students who have gone on to excel in science graduate schools and scientific careers. More meaningful contributions can be made in many cases in the professional lives of these students compared to the "A" students. This value-added component of undergraduate research represents one of its most notable attributes.

In their summer research experience, chemistry students can expect to work one-on-one with their faculty mentors as laboratory colleagues. The nature of this student-faculty interaction is a distinctive part of the department's approach to undergraduate research and is fundamental to the documented success of that approach. The summer students work side-by-side with their professors every day of the week for hours at a time, benefiting from continuous feedback and on-the-spot instruction, criticism and practical advice. In this format, students are viewed and treated as junior colleagues in the exciting process of scientific discovery and interpretation. Each spring the department hosts an academic fair where all research students present their research results on campus in a poster format. Invited guests include family members of the students, local high school teachers, chemistry and other faculty, administrators, representatives from local companies, and chemistry students who have not yet started their research activities. The research presentations provide another speaking opportunity for the seniors and serve to generate interest in the program among chemistry students enrolled in the lower-level courses. During their senior year, the students' research posters are prominently displayed in attractive wall cabinets throughout the hallways of the chemistry department. Group pictures of the summer research participants for the past twenty-one years are also displayed in a prominent fashion in the department.

RECOMMENDATIONS FOR UNDERGRADUATE RESEARCH

Research is an inherent component of chemistry, and a student's education in chemistry must be considered incomplete without research experience during the undergraduate years.

All participants . . . agreed about the importance of research for undergraduates, even at the expense of formal course work. Research was seen as a way to enable students to understand the the science . . . better, to become better scientists themselves, to identify with a group and a common goal, and to help in career decisions. . . .

Further advantages of a research experience . . . include seeing the relevance and applications of principles and techniques learned in traditional coursework, an increase in employability, and enhanced motivation and interest.

A quality undergraduate research experience requires immersion in a genuine research project in a well-equipped laboratory in a professional collaboration with a conscientious scientist-mentor.

The faculty mentors must be enthusiastic about their projects and interested in the outcome, set realistic expectations of time and effort, consider the level of the students' background, design suitable, segmented projects, encourage the students' feelings of ownership and pride in their projects, . . . make time for student contact, and provide opportunities for group interaction and . . . presentations. The mentor should make an effort to allow students some freedom in designing projects and making decsions, while at the same time guiding them toward an ultimate goal. The mentor should be a confidence-builder, possessing qualities of patience and the ability to offer encouragement in spite of setbacks. The experience should in the end be fun. The student should be made to feel an important component of a group effort.

—"Report on the NSF Workshop on Research in the Undergraduate Curriculum," NSF Division of Chemistry, 1991[1]

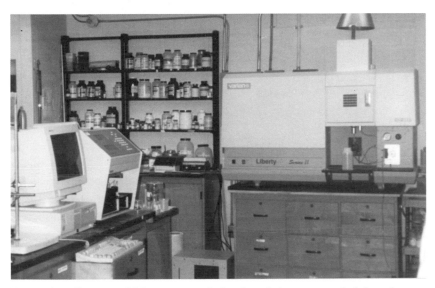

Furman's well-equipped laboratories include a liquid chromatograph, left, and an inductively coupled plasma-atomic emission spectrometer, center.

The research program includes more than just an intense effort in the laboratory. Over the years, social and sporting events have contributed to the mix of experiences enjoyed by the faculty and undergraduate research participants. Premier among these have been the "Iron Man" and "Iron Woman" challenges, each comprised of a series of seven sports competitions hotly contested by faculty and students alike. These organized games, which extend throughout the summer, present a wonderful opportunity for students to become acquainted with faculty in a most informal setting.

Laboratory equipment: A dual-use strategy

Another foundation for the department's success has been its ability to acquire instrumental and technical support facilities. The department maintains a collection of chemical instrumentation worth more than $3 million, some of which is listed in the table on page 126. Financial support from many different sources has been used in the purchase of this equipment, 82 percent of which has been obtained in the last ten years. Fund-raising efforts and purchasing decisions have targeted major equipment items that can serve both the needs of individual laboratory courses and the research requirements of every faculty member. Experiments in most (but not all) upper-level laboratories have been intentionally designed to use the same instrumentation required by the faculty to conduct their research programs. This plan works well provided there is sufficient breadth from a pedagogical perspective in the equipment items used and procedures for sharing are well formulated. Tremendous savings in faculty time, laboratory space and financial costs can be realized by such a coordinated arrangement. Also, the students benefit because they are able to conduct experiments with a greater variety of advanced instrumentation than would otherwise be possible. In addition, such dual-use equipment is more likely to be in good working order throughout the year because faculty have a vested interest in its maintenance. Obviously, this approach would not work well in a departmental setting in which upper-level laboratory courses are offered to a large number of students several times a year.

The department has avoided expensive service contracts (which are practically unaffordable anyhow) on most major equipment items by adopting a team approach to preventative maintenance and emergency repairs. Chemistry faculty members have various levels of expertise with computer-controlled instrumentation, lasers, electronics, cryogenics, optics, high vacuum equipment, etc. By pooling our individual talents and sharing the time burden required to obtain phone help from equipment manufacturers, major repair costs have been limited. The science division at Furman is also fortunate to have two technical support positions which are staffed by highly talented and helpful individuals. One manages the electronics and machine shop while the other has special computer skills.

The chemistry department occupies approximately 22,000 square feet in the Plyler Hall of Science, which was constructed in 1958 and enlarged in 1968. This old building literally hums with activity and the sounds of new equipment, some of which is located in recently renovated rooms. In addition to regular grant applications and university support, earnings from a departmental endowment fund are used to update and replace equipment in a timely manner.

The funding of instruments: Unique partnerships

In the late 1960s and throughout the 1970s most of the department's research equipment was homemade or obtained from government surplus and donations of out-of-date items from local companies. Yet the faculty demonstrated a talent at pursuing publishable science "on a shoestring," and these modest beginnings set the stage for the well-equipped position the department finds itself in today. Lon Knight's first electron spin resonance (ESR) matrix isolation apparatus was largely homemade, constructed in the local machine shop with student help. From results obtained on such primitive equipment he was able to secure external funding for commercial state-of-the-art cryostats and ESR spectrometers in a series of research project grant awards from the Physical Chemistry Section of NSF's Chemistry Division between 1976 and 1998. Noel Kane-Maguire began his studies of inorganic photosystems with a spectrofluorimeter largely built from components also obtained on surplus; his accomplishments with such relatively crude instrumentation helped support efforts to equip his laboratory for modern photochemical studies. His laboratory now includes several commercial spectro-fluorimeters, as well as instruments for measuring excited-state lifetimes and carrying out electrogenerated chemiluminescence.

Of particular assistance in these advances was NSF's equipment program for two- and four-year institutions (the old 69A program). The department received six equipment awards from this source over a relatively short period in the late 1970s and early 1980s. Similar success attended the department's application for equipment under NSF's Instrument and Laboratory Improvement (ILI) program. In this case, the pedagogical goals of that NSF program coincided nicely with the department's educational philosophy: modern instrumentation was incorporated as an integral part of classroom and laboratory instruction at Furman; in addition, the educational value of the undergraduate research facilitated by that instrumentation was both recognized and encouraged by the NSF. Research had not only become a vital part of the chemistry curriculum, but the need for expertise in instrument use and spectral interpretation served as a major incentive to accentuate those features in course work.

The Milliken Foundation is a trust established in 1945 and sponsored by Milliken and Company. The Foundation contributes only to preselected organizations. Higher education is included among their varied fields of interest.

By the late 1980s and early '90s, the department had advanced beyond dependence on straightforward sources of funding such as the NSF-ILI program. As examples of the new directions which were pursued, the Keck Foundation was successfully approached for a major share of the cost of the department's first superconducting NMR spectrometer. In a later initiative, the Milliken Foundation instituted a novel challenge grant that spurred the acquisition of funds from alumni and corporate sources used for the preparation and equipping of the department's laboratory for computational methods. As a final example, in 1989 when the Kresge Foundation solicited applications through its Science Initiative Program for funds to establish endowments for instrument purchases and replacement, Furman's chemistry program was one of the first to submit a successful application, even though the grant required a three-to-one match. With aggressive departmental fund-raising, that goal was achieved, and the department is now the beneficiary of the annual earnings of a $1.8 million endowment.

Sebastian S. Kresge, founder of the S.S. Kresge Company (now Kmart) established the Kresge Foundation in 1924. The foundation makes grants to build and renovate facilities, challenge private giving and build institutional capacity among nonprofit organizations. Their Science Initiative is a challenge-grant program to upgrade and endow scientific equipment.

Departmental efforts alone would not have been sufficient to meet this ambitious challenge from the Kresge Foundation. Decisions were made at the highest levels of the administration to allocate some major unrestricted gifts to the university in order to satisfy the Kresge challenge conditions and thus help establish this extremely important chemistry program fund. Aided in part by the successful acquisition and significant impact of this first Kresge Challenge Grant, a second Kresge challenge was awarded to the departments of computer science, physics, and mathematics in response to their joint grant proposal. Commitments of such high levels of matching support from the university have thus made an enormous impact on the science programs at Furman and have served as a significant boost to faculty morale. This fortunate circumstance continues to the present time.

One incident that occurred in the late 1980s under the presidency of Dr. John E. Johns illustrates how generous such matching can be. The chemistry department had approached several major funding sources for financial support in the purchase of our first high-field NMR instrument. Substantial university matching funds were made available to the department even though they were not absolutely required by these outside agencies. Fortunately, the department was successful in all of the major grants, and sufficient funds were accumulated to purchase the instrument without the need for university matching. Even in response to this remarkable success, the university made

President Johns congratulated the chemistry faculty for their aggressive efforts in fund-raising, and told them to consider the matching funds as a "reward."

available to the department the originally promised NMR matching funds (approximately $120,000) for the purchase of other equipment needs in support of the undergraduate research program. President Johns congratulated the chemistry faculty for the department's aggressive efforts in fund-raising, and told them to consider the matching funds as a "reward" to be used for those equipment needs which would be most beneficial to the program. Administrative support of this type and magnitude affects an academic program at a much more profound level than that indicated by the actual dollars involved!

Student recruitment

Student recruitment reflects the chemistry program's emphasis on undergraduate research. Beginning in the early 1970s, the recruitment of talented high school science students was established as a departmental priority. This tradition has been significantly strengthened, and the direct investment of time by the chemistry faculty in student recruitment is considered to be a major reason for the success of the chemistry program. Working closely with the university's admissions office, chemistry faculty members send prospective students information on the department's curriculum, areas of research, major equipment, and data on the national ranking of the program. The undergraduate research program is described and a group photograph of participants in the most recent summer research program is included (page 117). After the prospective students (80 to 120 at this stage) receive the information packet, personal phone calls are made to them by members of the chemistry faculty. The research group photograph is reported to be a distinctive marker that helps prospective students remember the Furman information among all the other college recruitment material they receive.

Visits are hosted by chemistry faculty and provide a wonderful opportunity to "show off " the laboratory equipment and to discuss the various undergraduate research opportunities.

During the recruitment period, information about chemistry scholarships is also sent to prospective chemistry majors. The availability of departmentally-awarded scholarships for incoming students is a major factor in encouraging students and their families to visit the campus and the chemistry department. These visits are hosted by chemistry faculty and provide a wonderful opportunity to "show off " the laboratory equipment and to discuss the various undergraduate research opportunities available in

113

the department. Funding for these scholarship awards is provided by an endowment gift to the department in the late 1960s by the Camille and Henry Dreyfus Foundation, ongoing support from the Dow Chemical Company Foundation, matching scholarship funding from the university, and three specialized scholarship endowment funds for women chemistry majors from South Carolina as well as for other potential chemistry majors planning specific career paths. The individual amounts of these eight departmental scholarships vary from about $1,000 to $4,000 annually; these awards are in addition to any financial assistance a student may receive from university sources.

An important factor in the recruitment of students is simply the department's track record. Just as certain undergraduate colleges become "pipelines" to particular graduate schools, so specific high school chemistry teachers direct many of their best students to Furman, based on the experiences and achievements of their former students. During the summer, high school chemistry teachers from across the state receive Advanced Placement (AP) course training in the chemistry department. A deliberate effort is made to expose the teachers to the various student-faculty research projects in our program. Typically, five Furman chemistry faculty members present talks on their research to the high school teachers, and the teachers tour various laboratories. They are also guests at the chemistry corporate luncheon, where they are introduced to all in attendance.

Establishing a sustainable financial base for undergraduate research: The importance of departmental fund-raising

In addition to ideas, programs, facilities and well-trained, dedicated people, it is essential that small college science departments engage in numerous avenues of fund-raising. For a research-oriented department financial support is so strongly linked to success that the department is well-advised to operate its own "development operation" in coordination with university-wide fund-raising activities. Conducting publishable and competitive science in the small-college setting is a difficult challenge from a financial perspective. Even if faculty secure individual, peer-reviewed research grants from external agencies on a regular basis, the amount is generally not sufficient to cover postdoctoral colleagues or the costs associated with the purchase and upkeep of essential, major equipment items. When traditional grants provide for the initial purchase of a major item, the maintenance and eventual replacement costs

114

are not included. In most colleges, institutional funds are also not available for the purchase or replacement of such major equipment items. A science department interested in establishing a record of research accomplishments must secure ongoing revenue streams (of a discretionary nature) from a variety of sources to meet these fundamental research needs. It is also important that budgetary procedures allow for the long-term accumulation and carry-over of funds in order to save for major projects in the future.

Professor Lon Knight, Furman's chemistry chair since 1981, has described his department's ongoing efforts to fund undergraduate research and its related needs in an article "Undergraduate Research and Departmental Fund-Raising."[2] The following excerpt from this article conveys the general strategy that has been developed at Furman:

> Student-faculty undergraduate research activities at a small college or large university can be coordinated into a departmental program and marketed as a premium product. In turn, this capitalistic approach can provide the financial means for improving departmental programs and maintaining the undergraduate research-rich environment when external support from traditional grant sources cannot meet increasing demands. Student scholarships and scientific instruments for use in both teaching and research endeavors can also be supported. Success in such departmental marketing (fund-raising activities) is more likely to result when it can be clearly demonstrated that the college or university is already meeting its obligation to support the academic programs.

The concept is simple and straightforward. Describe the scientific achievements, convey the excitement and genuine enthusiasm of these efforts, cite the evidence for educational effectiveness associated with undergraduate research to every conceivable audience on a regular basis and be bold in asking for their financial support. Academic departments should be able to raise needed financial support with a "winning" attitude and solid record of achievement, just as athletic departments have done for such a long time. While none of these fund-raising activities is especially creative, the keys to their successful deployment are execution, follow-through and fanatical persistence! Enthusiastic cooperation and professional help from the university's development office has been extremely valuable to our departmental fund-raising efforts over a long time period.

Alumni contributions

Furman has approximately 800 living chemistry alumni, the majority of whom participated in undergraduate research under the direction of Furman faculty. Solicitation letters are not sent on a routine basis to these alumni. However, the chemistry department does issue special appeals for specific challenge projects, and where appropriate, these requests are followed by personalized thank-you letters. Alumni are asked to support student stipends for summer research, supplies and special equipment, but never faculty stipends. In some years as many as fifteen out of the forty students conducting summer research are supported by alumni contributions. Successful alumni challenges over the past eight years have made substantial contributions towards the purchase of the 500 MHz NMR, the AFM/STM microscope, and computer equipment for the molecular modeling laboratory. Our most ambitious alumni challenge will be the planned creation of twenty permanently-endowed summer research student stipends, which will require, at current rates, approximately $1 million. We have already been able to establish four of these endowments and expect a major foundation's challenge to our alumni to enable the completion of this goal within the next ten years.

Alumni contacts help in many other areas as well, such as student recruitment, as valuable influences on the university decision makers, industrial ties (including the initiation of joint research projects and corporate contributions), and in locating internships and employment opportunities for our chemistry graduates. Beginning in 1994 the first chemistry alumni newsletter, organized and edited by Professor Laura Wright, was distributed; the third edition was recently published.

Corporate contributions and the corporate luncheon

Each year as many as fifteen local corporations make valuable financial contributions to our chemistry program. Included in this group are small, locally owned businesses and local operations of large multinational corporations. An informal annual report, including a summer research group photograph and a donation request for approximately $5,000, is sent to some thirty local companies each year. The photograph (which typically includes fifty to sixty students and faculty, page 117) is extremely important in personalizing the program. The univer-

Furman University Chemistry Department: Summer Research Program 1999.

sity president and academic dean are usually in the group photograph and are identified in the accompanying caption. The participation of these top administrators helps to convey to the corporate audience the university's high regard for the research program.

Chemistry's annual corporate luncheon is held on campus each summer, with expenses covered jointly by the chemistry and development departments. Typically three representatives from as many as twenty-five companies attend, including the CEO, the human resources director and the laboratory director or a staff scientist. Other guests include the university president and trustees, the academic dean, the chemistry faculty, visiting high school science teachers, faculty representatives from other science departments, foundation officials, selected chemistry alumni and, most importantly, all fifty summer research students.

This festive gathering of approximately 150 enthusiastic folks serves many useful purposes. Above all else, it leaves a lasting impression of the vitality and importance of undergraduate research among all present. The guests are seated in groups of eight at round tables displaying corporate signs, with carefully planned mixtures of corporate representatives, chemistry students and faculty members at each table. The occasion provides a showcase for "displaying" the students, describing the departmental research program and its operating costs, and "bragging" about its accomplishments to an interested and influential constituency. Departmental reports which include a list of equipment items and faculty research interests are also distributed.

Through the years, we have found that the luncheon is important for several other unanticipated reasons. A representative from each company is allotted about one minute to describe the nature and scope of its business. These presentations are interesting to everyone and often produce some good-natured sparring between competitive companies. Sometimes companies discover other firms that might be potential customers for their goods and services. It is also helpful for students who are making career plans to learn firsthand what these companies actually do. Another important part of the program is a brief presentation by one chemistry student from each faculty research group. Following the luncheon, students, faculty and corporate representatives engage in informal conversations. During the course of these various exchanges, they often discover areas of mutual scientific interest, and several of these encounters have led to productive collaborations that continue to provide financial support to the chemistry department.

Another corporate luncheon event is the introduction of our industrial liaison who holds a Ph.D. in analytical chemistry. The liaison solves simple problems for companies who call for help and coordinates solutions by utilizing the special expertise of other faculty. This no-charge service helps to keep the department in touch with the technical and equipment needs of local companies.

Following the luncheon, which is kept to ninety minutes (we eat and talk at the same time), optional tours of the chemistry department are offered. These events and the relationships that often emerge from them have helped to produce considerable financial support for the chemistry program and have significantly strengthened our interactions with local industry. For example, one local company recently provided $150,000 for the purchase of an inductively coupled plasma (ICP) instrument for trace elemental analysis and $80,000 for the creation of an endowed summer research scholarship.

Endowment earnings and internal support

The chemistry department at Furman is indeed fortunate to control the expenditure of earnings from several endowment accounts. The university has been most supportive in maintaining regular budget support despite the existence of such endowment income. In response to a $300,000 challenge from the Kresge Foundation in 1989, the department has now accumulated a $1.8 million endowment for major equipment purchases and replacements. Other endowments support four student research stipends each summer; the endowments for the J. A. Southern Lectureship and the J. R. Sampey Fund for Undergraduate Research honor former chemistry faculty members who made major contributions to the early development of Furman's chemistry program. The costs associated with sending students to present talks at various scientific meetings are also supported by departmental endowments. Several endowed scholarships designated for intended chemistry majors are especially important in the recruitment of outstanding high school science students.

In addition to matching contributions, the university provides support for student-faculty research through the annual departmental budget, which has equipment and maintenance components. Through its Furman Advantage Program, the university funds forty summer research stipends for students in all academic disciplines. The Advantage Program is modeled after chemistry's undergraduate research program and was initially funded in 1985 by a grant from the Charles A. Dana Foundation. It is part of a larger strategic initiative referred to as "engaged learning" which has been unanimously adopted by the trustees, administration and faculty. The stipends of three to five summer research students in chemistry are typically funded each year by the Furman Advantage Program. Through this program the university also funds, in a competitive manner, eight summer research stipends among faculty in all academic disciplines. To be eligible, the faculty must conduct research with students on a full-time basis for at least ten weeks in the summer.

Established in 1950 by Charles A. Dana, a New York State legislator and industrialist, the Dana Foundation's principal interests are currently in neuroscience and primary education. Prior to 1992, their activities included support of private higher education at four-year liberal arts colleges.

Foundation support

The chemistry program has had unusual success over the years in obtaining major departmental grants from a variety of foundations and corporations. Since the mid-1980s these sources have included twenty-six different agencies, with nine grants from local organizations. One of the most recent awards was from the Arnold and Mabel Beckman Foundation under their Beckman Scholars Program for 1999–2000. These awards have supported the undergraduate research program, student scholarships, faculty additions and the purchase of research instruments. In almost every case the effectiveness of these grants has been significantly increased by generous university matching funds, even in those situations where matching was not required by the external agency.

Funding for undergraduate research and related needs at Furman in the 1960s and 1970s came almost exclusively from NSF's Undergraduate Research Participation (URP) grants, a departmental development grant from Research Corporation and a small number of individual faculty awards. The department has received URP or Research Experiences for Undergraduates (REU; see page 192) site grants every year that these programs have been offered by NSF. Our most recent REU renewal application has been funded for $165,000 over the period 1999–2001. The temporary termination of NSF's URP program from 1980 to 1984 forced us to develop alternative funding sources for our departmental program of undergraduate research in chemistry. The growth in the research program and the need for reliable and more diverse sources of support are the primary reasons why various fund-raising strategies exist in Furman's chemistry department today. During the academic year 1997–1998, chemistry faculty were awarded $655,000 in external research project support and $224,000 in research instrumentation grants, not including university matching contributions. While these specific amounts are higher than those procured in previous, more typical years, our trend towards increasing external support is well established.

Faculty research grants

Nothing is more important to initiating and maintaining funding for undergraduate research than peer-reviewed research awards to faculty members. Chemistry faculty members have consistently been successful in obtaining grants from sources such as the NSF, Research Corporation, the Department of Energy, National Institutes of Health and the Petroleum Research Fund, but each faculty member will not have an outside grant every year. This is a reality that must be recognized by the department and university so that local support can be provided to keep an individual from losing his or her research momentum. Overcoming this difficulty is one of the most important uses of departmental discretionary funds! The percentage of the nine chemistry faculty members who have had external research project funding in a given year has varied between 70 and 100 percent (over the past ten years). Our departmental culture has been to encourage and help each other apply for research grants and to support colleagues who are between grants. The

Our departmental culture has been to encourage and help each other apply for research grants.

critical reading of a colleague's proposal is a major responsibility that has been accepted by the entire group.

Achievement indicators: Students and faculty

The quality and vitality of any departmental program are characteristics difficult to quantify, but there are a number of objective measurements which can help to verify achievement. Program growth, in terms of numbers of faculty, majors and support staff, is one such indicator. In all of these categories Furman's chemistry department has seen significant increases. Similarly, the remarkable increase in equipment holdings provides another tangible indication of growth—one which encompasses quality as well as size.

The total student population in all chemistry courses has doubled over the past twenty years to approximately 1000 student-course enrollments annually—a rate that exceeds the overall university growth. The department has averaged twenty-five chemistry graduates per year over the past ten years with 49 percent pursuing graduate degrees in chemistry, 26 percent enrolling in medical or dental school, and 10 percent taking industrial positions. Of 245 chemistry graduates in this time period, 119 have entered graduate school in chemistry, biochemistry or related fields, and another sixty-two have begun medical or dental school. Data from *Chemical and Engineering News* show that since 1991 Furman has ranked among the top four undergraduate institutions in the number of ACS-Committee on Professional Training (CPT; see page 122) certified B.S. degrees awarded in chemistry.[3] Significant progress has been made in this category since we were in thirtieth position in 1989 and rose to twelfth position in 1990. Although data from the ACS is not yet reported, the classes of 1997 through 2000 have also included twenty-five to thirty-five certified chemistry graduates.

According to data on baccalaureate origins of doctoral recipients in chemistry compiled by the National Research Council for the time period for 1983 to 1992, Furman's chemistry department ranked ninth

The ACS Committee on Professional Training

Established in 1936, the American Chemical Society Committee on Professional Training facilitates the maintenance and improvement of the quality of education in chemistry. The members are selected to maintain a balanced representation of the subdisciplines of chemistry, representation of liberal arts colleges, research universities, and the chemical industry.

The committee develops and administers the guidelines of the ACS for chemistry departments in colleges and universities that prepare undergraduate students for employment as professional chemists, for entrance into graduate school in chemistry and related fields, and for employment in which a strong background in chemistry is needed. The CPT is also responsible for the publication of the ACS Directory of Graduate Research and conducts surveys to monitor trends, developments, and problems in chemical education.

The CPT strongly endorses undergraduate research as one of the most rewarding aspects of the undergraduate experience. They believe that "research can integrate the components of the core curriculum into a unified picture and help [students] acquire a spirit of inquiry, independence, sound judgment, and persistence. By doing research, undergraduates develop the ability to use the chemical literature and report effectively in spoken and written presentations. . . . Supervison of research helps the faculty maintain enthusiasm, professional competence, and scholarly productivity."[4]

nationally among predominantly undergraduate institutions as a source of chemistry Ph.D.s.[5] Currently, more than sixty Furman chemistry graduates are enrolled in Ph.D. programs at institutions including MIT, Stanford, Yale, Chicago, Caltech, Florida, Virginia, Duke, Indiana, North Carolina, Kansas, Vanderbilt and Utah.

These Furman chemistry graduates have been noteworthy in terms of quality as well as quantity. Over the past ten years, eight have earned NSF graduate fellowships, one has been awarded a Fulbright Fellowship and two have received the Goldwater Scholarship. Similarly informative are data on student activity in presenting the results of their research studies. The department routinely pays the expenses of a contingent of eighteen to twenty-five students who present their results at regional ACS meetings. Commonly, the number of Furman chemistry students presenting talks at the annual Southeast Regional ACS meeting exceeds that of any other institution, including those with Ph.D. programs. Over the last three years, Furman chemistry students have presented seventy-eight papers at regional and national meetings. Moreover, undergraduate research participants are frequently involved in the publication process: over the past five years, a total of seventy-nine papers have been published by Furman faculty, with 125 Furman students included as co-authors for an average of 1.8 papers per faculty per year. This level of research productivity compares well with the national average of 1.3 papers per year for colleges with active research programs.

Faculty accomplishments manifest themselves in a number of ways, including those resulting from a willingness to take advantage of changing circumstances. Two of the current staff, originally trained as organometallic chemists, moved into areas of more contemporary interest as those opportunities arose—Tim Hanks into materials chemistry, and Laura Wright into surface science. As student interests began to gravitate to areas removed from classical chemistry, the research interests of several faculty began to include topics related to both biochemistry and environmental chemistry. The department took advantage of the opportunity for a cooperative venture with Los Alamos National Laboratory under the able leadership of Tony Arrington. From 1991 to 1999, forty chemistry majors from Furman have conducted research at Los Alamos under the direction of Professor Arrington and staff scientists at the laboratory. Cooperative arrangements with Milliken and Company and Columbia University's Biosphere 2 project are now being established by a number of the chemistry faculty.

The professional activities of the chemistry faculty have also garnered national recognition: one has won the ACS Award for Research at an Undergraduate Institution; three have served on the Science Advancement Programs Advisory Committee of Research Corporation; a number have been on review panels for NSF, NIH, and the Camille and Henry Dreyfus Foundation; two have received Dreyfus Teacher-Scholar Awards, and three have received Dreyfus Scholar/Fellow Awards. One has served on the advisory panel for the Chemistry Division of NSF; another was a founding councilor of the Council for Undergraduate Research, and a third currently serves in that capacity. The faculty are equally dedicated in their classroom teaching role: three current and one retired chemistry faculty member have won the annual university award for teaching excellence, a record equaled by only one other department on campus.

Two former faculty members, after having made major contributions to our chemistry program, went on to positions of national prominence.

These were R. Scott Pyron (Furman years, 1966–76) who has had a distinguished career at Research Corporation and Research Corporation Technologies, and William C. Harris (1971–77) who went to NSF as a temporary program official and rose to the level of assistant director. Bill was the president of Biosphere 2, operated under the auspices of Columbia University, before returning to the University of South Carolina as Vice President for Research. Another former chemistry faculty member, T. R. Nanney (1960–67), started Furman's computer center and the department of computer science. Since 1969, he has been a distinguished professor in that discipline at Furman.

The future

In a real sense, the challenge for the future will be to remain on the proven and exciting path of the past with faculty-student research as the focus of the educational program. This ambition is by no means a static or stagnant one since the goals, areas and challenges of research are constantly changing. Having faculty members who are willing to tap the dynamic excitement of this ever-changing landscape is a great way to insure inspirational and effective science "teaching." Therefore our vision for the future is to retain dedicated, creative and productive scientists as the teaching faculty in the chemistry department, to recruit talented science students who can best benefit from such unusual opportunities, and to secure the financial means and facilities to operate the program at the highest possible level.

Several projects are planned to improve the chemistry program and further develop its potential for working with students as junior colleagues. To help fulfill this vision, a new $20 million science building is planned which will house biochemistry, molecular biology and other areas of chemistry and biology that have begun to merge over recent years. Existing science space will be renovated to accommodate other areas of chemistry, physics, biology, and earth and environmental science (geology). A special design feature in both of these projects will be the creation of space ideally suited for undergraduate research and other types of engaged learning activities, and other renovations which will foster jointly-sponsored activities among these natural science disciplines. We are also planning to increase the level of joint academic-industrial projects and to accommodate these new research opportunities in the building renovation.

New strategies need to be developed for expanding our interactions with local high school science teachers, for acquiring more chemistry scholarship funds, and for developing new recruiting methods to attract the best students in the region. One of our most important challenges will be securing endowment funds to insure the continuation of the summer research program. New laboratory experiments that can take full advantage of the recent acquisitions of major equipment need to be designed for the chemistry courses in the major's sequence. In the immediate future, we plan to purchase a scanning electron microscope (SEM) and additional GC/MS equipment; laboratory renovation and the purchase of modern equipment for teaching the principles and applications of lasers are already underway. Cost-sharing plans with industrial partners for the joint use of these and other major equipment items need to be developed. Also, we envision that shared equipment will facilitate the development of scientific projects of mutual academic-industrial interest and create more applied research opportunities for faculty and students.

The exciting growth and development of Furman's chemistry program has benefited immensely from the inspiration, ideas and procedures of generous and helpful colleagues at other institutions. For a successful future, Furman's faculty must continue to interact with and learn from colleagues across the country. Science faculty members everywhere need to convince their constituencies and the public at large that we produce the only "product" capable of solving the technological challenges and managing the opportunities that lie ahead. The higher the quality of training and education the scientific leaders of tomorrow receive, the richer and the more rewarding life will be for everyone. Æ

Major Equipment in Furman's Chemistry Department for Undergraduate Instruction and Research (January 1999)

	Cost	Purchased
MAGNETIC RESONANCE		
Varian Inova 500 High-Field Superconducting NMR Spectrometer	$454,000	1996
Varian VXR-300S High-Field Super-conducting NMR Spectrometer	329,000	1989
Varian EM-360A Proton NMR Spectrometer	31,000	1981
Varian E-109 ESR Spectrometer (2)	120,000	1979
Bruker ESR Spectrometer ERD 200	144,000	1988
Bruker ESR Spectrometer ECS 106	110,000	1992
Hewlett Packard Microwave Frequency Counter Model	14,000	1995
LASERS		
Spectra-Physics 4 Watt Argon Ion Laser	$25,000	1990
Spectra-Physics PDL-2 Pulsed Dye Laser	36,000	1988
Molectron Pulsed Nitrogen Laser	15,000	1979
Molectron Dye Laser System DL-14	26,000	1981
Nd:YAG Laser Spectra Physics	65,000	1985
Spectra Physics DCR-11 Nd:YAG Laser (2)	68,000	1988
Lumonics 505 Excimer Laser	42,000	1992
Coherent Innova 90 - 5W Argon Ion Laser	24,000	1996
Coherent CR-599 Dye Laser	15,000	1996
MASS SPECTROMETERS		
GC/MS Hewlett-Packard 5970	$78,000	1985
EAI 250 Quadrupole Mass Spectrometer (3)	12,000	1984
R.M. Jordon Co. TOF Reflectron MS	36,000	1988
R.M. Jordon Co. Quadrupole MS	12,000	1989
Stanford Research Systems RGA Quadrupole Mass Spectrometer (2)	14,000	1996
ELECTROCHEMICAL EQUIPMENT		
Princeton Applied Research (PAR) System	$20,000	1980
Princeton Applied Research (PAR) System	13,000	1988/1990

	Cost	Purchased
ELECTROCHEMICAL EQUIPMENT (cont.)		
Bio Analytical Systems 100 B/W Electrochemical Workstations (2)	$55,000	1994
Bio Analytical Systems LC-4 Amperometric Controllers (2)	12,000	1994
SEPARATIONS EQUIPMENT		
Varian 5060 Ternary Gradient LC(2)	$ 34,500	1980
Hewlett-Packard 1090L Liquid Chromatograph with Diode-Array Detector and 3362 Work Station	42,600	1987
Varian 4600 Gas Chromatograph (2)	8,000	1980
Varian 3700 Gas Chromatograph	10,000	1981
Hewlett-Packard 5890A Capillary GC (3)	12,400	1985
Spectra-Physics 500 - Capillary Electrophoresis System (CES)	21,000	1992
HP 1050 LC with UV detection	30,000	1992
Spectra-Physics 1000 CES	35,000	1992
Supercritical Fluid Extractor	15,000	1992
Gas Chromatograph (HP 5890)	10,000	1992
P/ACE System 5000 CES	30,000	1996
P/ACE System 5500 CES	35,000	1997
Beckman MDQ CES	45,000	1999
Dionex Ion Chromatograph	25,000	1999
COMPUTERS		
Apple PowerMacs Modeling System (10)	$50,000	1998
CAChe Stereo Modeling Systems (2)	60,000	1992
IBM RISC 6000/530H with Graphics Accelerator	75,000	1992
Silicon Graphics Indigo Workstation	14,000	1995
Silicon Graphics O_2 Workstation	15,000	1998
Hewlett Packard Kayak Workstation	5,000	1998
Micron Millennia Pro II Plus Workstation	4,000	1996

	Cost	Purchased
OPTICAL SPECTROSCOPY		
Nicolet Magna FTIR Spectrometer	$41,000	1993
Spex Raman Spectrometer	65,000	1998
Perkin-Elmer 1640 FT-IR	21,000	1988
Varian 2290 UV-Visible Spectrophotometer/ Multiscan System	33,600	1988
Perkin-Elmer 552 UV-Visible System	10,000	1980
Aminco-Bowman 48203D Spectrophotofluorimeter	8,500	1975
Hewlett-Packard Model 8452A Diode Array Spectrophotometer (2)	26,000	1990
Perkin-Elmer Paragon 500 FT-IR	14,000	1996
Spex Spectrofluorimeter Fluorolog-2	48,000	1996
SLM-8000 C Spectrophotofluorimeter	44,800	1990
JASCO CD J-710 Spectrophotometer	55,000	1991
Varian Liberty Series II Inductively Coupled Plasma–Atomic Emission Spectrometer	102,000	1998
Varian Cary 100 Bio UV-Visible System	15,000	1998
Varian Cary 50 Probe UV-Visible System	10,000	1998
Instrumentation Laboratory Model 551 AA	35,000	1980
MISCELLANEOUS INSTRUMENTS		
APD Liquid Helium 4 K Cryostat	$12,000	1984
APD Liquid Helium 4 K Cryostat	14,000	1987
APD Heliplex 4 K Closed Cycle Refrigerator	35,000	1984
APD Heliplex 4 K Closed Cycle Refrigerator	38,000	1988
CryoAmerica 4 K Helium Cryostat	9,000	1995
Peptide Synthesizer, Vega Biotechnologies Model 1000	15,000	1986
Perkin-Elmer 241 MC Polarimeter	24,000	1979

	Cost	Purchased
MISCELLANEOUS INSTRUMENTS (cont.)		
Biosystem PCR-Mate 391 DNA Synthesizer	$15,000	1990
Bio-Rad 620 Video Densitometer	20,000	1991
Perkin-Elmer DSC 7 Differential Scanning Calorimeter & TGA 7 Thermal Gravimetric Analyzer	65,000	1993
Zeiss Fluorescence and Polarizing Microscopes	20,000	1995
Digital Instruments Nanoscope III Scanning Probe Microscope	108,000	1996
Phillips MCN 101 X-ray Generator w/ MG161 Power Supply	35,000	1991
Veeco MS17 Helium Mass Spectrometric Leak Tester (2)	38,000	1988
LeCroy Digital Oscilloscope	12,000	1998
Vacuum Atmospheres Co. HE-243 Inert Atmosphere Box	30,000	1980
Molecular Beam High Vacuum System w/ 10" Diffusion Pump	45,000	1992

SECTION III
SUPPORTING EXCELLENCE

THERE IS NOTHING WHICH CAN
BETTER DESERVE OUR PATRONAGE
THAN THE PROMOTION OF SCIENCE
AND LITERATURE. KNOWLEDGE IS IN
EVERY COUNTRY THE SUREST BASIS
OF PUBLIC HAPPINESS.

— GEORGE WASHINGTON,
ADDRESS TO CONGRESS, 1790

IN A FUNDING COMPETITION in which slight differences in percentile rankings or priority scores are crucial, every aspect of the
grant application must be as strong as possible. *Especially* in cases
where the sponsoring institution is a less research-intensive school,
the research environment and the quality of the school's commitment to scientific research can be critical.

One of the most important messages that we wish to impart is
that there are many people who can provide useful information
and advice to a grant applicant. These include administrators at
the PI's school, faculty colleagues, scientific collaborators, and
NIH personnel. NIH funding is highly competitive, and whether
a PI chooses to prepare an application in isolation or with ample
input and feedback from these individuals can spell the difference
between failure and success in landing an NIH grant.

John M. Schwab is Program Director in Pharmacology,
Physiology, and Biological Chemistry at the NIGMS.

Jean Chin is Program Director in Cell Biology
and Biophysics at the NIGMS.

John M. Schwab and Jean Chin

9 NIH FUNDING: AN INSIDE GUIDE TO GRANTSMANSHIP

How can a faculty member from a smaller or non-research-intensive university or college find funding for his or her research? If a case can be made that the project is relevant to human health, either directly or indirectly, then the National Institutes of Health (NIH) is a logical first stop (http://www.nih.gov).

In this chapter, we will review the process for proposal preparation, submission, review, and funding. The discussion will be embellished with program staff advice as well as with examples of the types of comments reviewers might make, according to the following outline:

NIH research interests
NIH research grant mechanisms
Contacts before submission
Preparing a grant application
Submitting your application
Review process and review criteria
Receipt and referral of your application
Review and scoring
Revision and resubmission
Funding

NIH research interests

NIH is composed of over twenty institutes and centers (ICs; Table 1, page 134), most of which have the authority to award research grants. The ICs support a wide variety of research in such diverse fields as biology, chemistry, biochemistry, biophysics, computer sciences, bioengineering, mathematics, epidemiology, nutrition, and behavioral sciences. The feature that is common to all NIH-supported research is that it somehow can be related to the improvement of human health.

The primary mission of the National Institute of General Medical Sciences is to provide funding for basic scientific research.

Some NIH-supported projects are quite applied, however, others are best characterized as basic science. Among all of the ICs, the National Institute of General Medical Sciences (NIGMS) bears special mention, since its primary mission is to

TABLE I
NIH Institutes and Centers

NCI	National Cancer Institute
NEI	National Eye Institute
NHLBI	National Heart, Lung, and Blood Institute
NHGRI	National Human Genome Research Institute
NIA	National Institute on Aging
NIAAA	National Institute on Alcohol Abuse and Alcoholism
NIAID	National Institute of Allergy and Infectious Diseases
NIAMS	National Institute of Arthritis and Musculoskeletal and Skin Diseases
NICHD	National Institute of Child Health and Human Development
NIDCD	National Institute on Deafness and Other Communication Disorders
NIDCR	National Institute of Dental and Craniofacial Research
NIDDK	National Institute of Diabetes and Digestive and Kidney Diseases
NIDA	National Institute on Drug Abuse
NIEHS	National Institute of Environmental Health Sciences
NIGMS	National Institute of General Medical Sciences
NIMH	National Institute of Mental Health
NINDS	National Institute of Neurological Disorders and Stroke
NINR	National Institute of Nursing Research
NLM	National Library of Medicine
CC	Warren Grant Magnuson Clinical Center
CIT	Center for Information Technology
NCCAM	National Center for Complementary and Alternative Medicine
NCRR	National Center for Research Resources
FIC	John E. Fogarty International Center
CSR	Center for Scientific Review

provide funding for basic scientific research. To use chemistry as an example, while some NIGMS-supported projects have obvious relevance to human health (e.g., the synthesis and evaluation of HIV protease inhibitors), for many projects (e.g., synthetic methods development or host-guest chemistry) the relationship is far less direct. The same is true of NIGMS-supported research projects in biology, plant sciences, and behavioral sciences that focus on basic studies of prokaryotes and eukaryotes at a molecular, cellular, or organismal level. Such projects have potential utility for revealing general disease mechanisms or normal biological processes.

How can you find out if your project might be of interest to NIH? The first approach is to become familiar with the various ICs and their research interests, using links from the NIH Web site to the ICs' Web sites. Another is to search the CRISP database, http://commons.cit. nih.gov/ crisp/owa/CRISP.Generate_Ticket, which includes titles and abstracts for active NIH grants, to see whether projects similar to yours currently are supported. In this way, you may be able to determine whether the type of science for which you would like NIH funding is appropriate to NIH, as well as whether someone else is already funded to do your project! Another useful approach is to speak directly with NIH extramural program staff. The following URLs provide helpful starting points:

http://grants.nih.gov/grants/policy/emprograms/index.html
http://nigms.nih.gov/funding/funding.html
http://directory.nih.gov/

NIH research grant mechanisms

There is a rich history of NIH-funded research at smaller universities and colleges through the R15 (Academic Research Enhancement Award; AREA) program and the R01 mechanism for investigator-initiated research. These mechanisms are subject to many of the same criteria for evaluation, which will be discussed below. General information and guidelines for these programs, as well as application forms and answers to frequently asked questions may be accessed through the NIH Web sites listed above and in Table IV (page 154).

1. The AREA Program

The R15 Academic Research Enhancement Award program is an NIH-wide program to fund the meritorious research of principal investigators (PI; see Table II, page 136) at less research-intensive institutions.

Table II
Abbreviations Used in Text

AREA	Academic Research Enhancement Award (R15)
BNP	Bioorganic and Natural Products Study Section
CRISP	Database with information on NIH-funded research projects
CSR	Center for Scientific Review; reviews most NIH grant applications
IC	Institute or Center
IRG	Integrated Review Group; a cluster of individual study section panels
MCHA	Medicinal Chemistry Study Section
NIH	National Institutes of Health
PA	Program Announcement of IC interest in a specific area
PD	Program Director; makes funding recommendations and manages funded grants
PI	Principal Investigator
RFA	Request for Applications; announcement of programs for which an IC has set-aside funds
SRA	Scientific Review Administrator; organizes study section panels and prepares summary statements

The program was started in 1985 to give colleges and universities that have not benefited from extensive federal support the opportunity to participate in NIH-funded research. In recognition of the fact that many leading scientists are products of AREA-eligible, mostly undergraduate institutions, the AREA program is restricted to institutions that have received less than $2 million per year in total costs from NIH-funded research in at least four of the previous seven years. Preference is given to PIs who have a record of, or potential for, sending a significant number of students to graduate school in preparation for health science careers.

The three objectives of the AREA program are: providing support for meritorious research; strengthening the research environment at institutions that are not research-intensive; and exposing students at such institutions to meritorious research.

It is understood that investigators at smaller universities and liberal arts colleges tend to have heavy teaching loads during the academic year and that serious research activity may be limited to the summer months. Thus, the scope of a typical three-year AREA project will be smaller than that of a typical, four-year R01 research project.

An AREA grant provides a total of $100,000 (direct costs) over a one-, two-, or three-year project period to support mostly summer salary for the PI and undergraduate students, supplies, and travel to scientific meetings. PIs of AREA grants may also apply for supplements to support and train underrepresented minorities or disabled individuals in biomedical careers. R15 grants are made with funds provided by the NIH Office of the Director (OD), and not from funds that are used for R01 grants; thus, applicants do not compete directly against the laboratories at major research institutions. Although competition is among scientists at less research-intensive institutions, in recent years the overall funding for R15 grants has been somewhat limited, which has made the AREA program quite competitive (see Table III, page 138).

Information about the AREA program, previously funded AREA grants, review criteria, and a list of institutions excluded from AREA funding eligibility may be found at the AREA Web site: http://grants. nih.gov/grants/funding/area.htm.

2. The Investigator-Initiated Research Grant (R01) Program

Simply being at a smaller, less research-intensive school does not make one noncompetitive for an investigator-initiated R01 grant. For example, in the NIGMS chemistry portfolio as of 2000, faculty at nine R15-eligible schools held regular R01 grants for research in organic, bioorganic, or medicinal chemistry. These schools are Lehigh, Marquette, Montana State, North Dakota State, and West Virginia Universities; Rensselaer Polytechnic Institute; the Universities of Alabama (Tuscaloosa) and New Mexico; and the Pharmacy School at the University of Tennessee at Memphis. Indeed, both another author in this volume (Michael Doyle, while at Hope College and Trinity University) and one author of this chapter (J.M.S., while at the Catholic University of America) held R01 grants while teaching at smaller schools.

The R01 grants ordinarily provide three to five years of support (depending upon the NIH IC to which the application is assigned) and include the funds required to accomplish the project goals during that period of time. Typically, the budget will include funds for the PI's summer salary and a small percentage of the academic year salary; support of graduate students, postdoctoral fellows, or technicians; supplies; project-related travel; and other project-related expenses. Competition for R01 grants is stiff, since there is no formal limit on the scope of the project, the size of the budget that may be requested, or the size or mission of the applicant organization. Thus, projects from smaller labs staffed mostly by undergraduates are compared to projects from larger laboratories with

TABLE III

AREA: Applications and Awards Funded from all NIH Sources [1]

Fiscal Year	Number of Competing Applications	Number of Awards	Success Rate	Dollars Awarded (thousands)
1985	420	38	9.0	$ 2,515
1986	309	184	59.5	12,121
1987	371	152	41.0	9,835
1988	411	173	42.1	10,997
1989	720	115	16.0	11,319
1990	698	115	16.5	11,420
1991	614	139	22.6	13,721
1992	556	153	27.5	15,281
1993	510	128	25.1	12,911
1994	594	138	23.2	13,581
1995	582	140	24.1	13,845
1996	630	167	26.5	16,788
1997	650	164	25.2	16,277
1998	451	162	35.9	16,536
1999	441	174	39.5	17,634

numerous graduate students and postdoctoral fellows.

In short, the keys to success are an outstanding research idea, a strong presentation of that idea, the PI's expertise, and a commitment on the part of the institution to research as a central component of higher education. For a project from a smaller institution to be competitive, not only must the research problem be compelling, but the PI must be able to be address it satisfactorily with the resources and personnel that are available. Planning is critical, so that the demands of the project do not outstrip the available personnel, facilities, and equipment. Indeed, a good postdoctoral fellow can be the key to a successful project, particularly when graduate students are not available.

Contacts before submission

Suppose that you have an idea, but you have never written an NIH grant application. You've explored the relevant links at the NIH Web site, but you still have questions that are specific to your own particular project or institution. Depending on what type of information you need, there are three good sources of assistance.

Contact your sponsored research office. Formally, research grant applications are not submitted by the principal investigator, but instead by an institution (e.g., college or university) on behalf of the PI. Thus, the face page of the standard NIH application form (PHS 398) includes signature blocks for both the PI and an official signing on behalf of the applicant institution. Most universities have an "office of sponsored research" (or the equivalent), a major function of which is to facilitate the preparation and submission of grant applications and contract proposals. The office of sponsored research, or the business official who signs off on grant applications, can provide important information about the institution's procedures. Specifically, since the institution will be responsible for administering your grant, various institutional officials may need to approve of your application and budget before they are submitted. Is there an office that must be consulted in formulating the budget? How much budgetary detail will be needed by the institution prior to submission? Who needs to approve of your application, and how long will that take? The office of sponsored research can answer those questions and can help you obtain NIH forms, such as the PHS 398 application form, and copies of Program Announcements (PAs) and Requests for Applications (RFAs) from the *NIH Guide* (all of these items are also available on the NIH Web sites summarized in Table IV, page 154).

Involve your colleagues. Potentially the most useful source of information on all aspects of grant application preparation, project planning, and execution of the project are your faculty colleagues or collaborators. Ideally, these are individuals who have "been there and done that." They should be able to provide helpful advice about the mechanics of preparing and submitting a grant application, especially factors that are specific to your institution. They also will be invaluable sources of feedback as you polish your ideas and craft your grant application.

Regrettably, many new faculty members are reluctant to ask for help from their senior colleagues, and senior colleagues may be reluctant to offer assistance if it has not been requested. Sometimes a new faculty member will hesitate to "impose" on a senior colleague for fear that the debt cannot be repaid in kind. In this case, it is worthwhile to remember that although you are on the receiving end in your early days as a faculty member, you will have the opportunity in the future to provide advice and feedback to the next generation of junior colleagues.

Particularly at a smaller or less research-intensive, AREA-eligible school, you may not have any colleagues who have been successful in securing NIH funding. In this event, it would be wise to look beyond the confines of your own institution in seeking mentoring and feedback on your project and your grant application. Good alternative sources of input include former postdoctoral or graduate school mentors or colleagues,

It would be wise to look beyond your own institution in seeking mentoring on your project and grant application.

or colleagues with whom you have become acquainted from professional meetings. Once again, seek out mentors who have been successful in obtaining NIH funding. Another potentially useful approach is through a professional society. A growing number of these societies sponsor mentoring programs and grantsmanship workshops for young faculty researchers.

Speak with NIH staff. Another excellent way to obtain information on administrative aspects of grant application and review is to contact review or program staff at NIH. As mentioned above, the NIH Web site provides links to the ICs' home pages, from which you can access descriptions of research areas funded by each IC as well as the names of program directors (PDs) who manage grants in your area of interest. You can use the NIH Directory (http://directory.nih.gov/) to obtain telephone and e-mail information for PDs, who can verify the potential interest of the IC in your project or help you identify another IC that is more suitable. A PD can also recommend appropriate study sections for peer review of your application.

You can find contact information for study section Scientific Review Administrators (SRAs) at http://www.drg.nih.gov/committees/roster index.asp. An SRA can help you determine whether his or her study section is the most appropriate one to review your application and can also answer questions regarding the mechanics of peer review. If you have concerns that special expertise may be needed for the review of your application or that a member of the study section may have a conflict of interest, this should be discussed with the SRA.

Preparing a grant application

Give yourself time. Before you start preparing your grant application, make sure you budget enough time to do your best work. If it's New Year's Day and you haven't yet completed your literature work, don't aim for the January 25 deadline for R15 applications. Give your ideas time to mature—make sure you've thought about all the angles. Leave time to get feedback from colleagues and to address any suggestions that they may have.

Get outside opinions. In all aspects of preparing a grant application, the best advice is to not "do it in a vacuum." Even an experienced investigator can profit from discussing his or her project at an early stage with someone who can provide advice or constructive criticism, or from having a colleague read sections of the application to verify that the arguments are compelling and even that there are no obvious errors in grammar or spelling! For a new investigator, this sort of early feedback is essential, minimizing the frustration and delays that result from preventable mistakes as well as the potential harm that could result from exposing avoidable flaws to the scrutiny of peer reviewers.

Find a significant and high-impact research idea. Clearly, the most critical aspect of preparing a grant application is to come up with a good research idea. Your project should be one that suits your background and experience; it should be significant and creative; and it should be achievable with the resources (e.g., staffing, equipment, and lab space) that are available to you. The last point is especially significant for PIs at less research-intensive schools. If your school doesn't have the high-field NMR spectrometer or the analytical ultracentrifuge that is required for the project, then arrange for access at another institution and obtain a letter to that effect to include with your application. If your project involves some experiments that you aren't qualified to carry out, find a collaborator who does have the proper expertise. Include a letter of collaboration (describing the experimental approach to be taken) and a copy of your collaborator's

Your project should be one that suits your background and experience.

biographical sketch in your application. In fact, interdisciplinary research projects can be very innovative and often will be quite appealing to both peer reviewers and NIH ICs, particularly if the science is truly synergistic and will lead to insights that could not result from a more narrow approach. If you do propose an interdisciplinary project, make certain that your part is clearly identifiable and that it showcases your intellectual contribution to the project. Finally, make sure to get ample input from your collaborator(s) during the preparation of your application.

Read a successful grant application. Any PI who has not yet garnered independent NIH support should make a serious effort to read one or more successful applications prior to writing his or her own. Try to identify and emulate those features that make successful applications easy to read and understand. Former mentors and colleagues are good sources for such applications.

Obtain the correct application forms. Once you have come up with an idea, done extensive literature research, formulated an experimental approach, and read some good grant applications, it is time to begin writing. The application form for most NIH grants (including R01 and R15 grants) is known as the PHS 398. A hard copy version of the PHS 398 is likely to be available from your sponsored research office (see *Contact your sponsored research office*, above). It can also be read and printed (in pdf format) from the NIH Web site: http://grants.nih.gov/grants/funding/phs398/phs398.html. Many applicants, however, prefer to use electronic versions of the PHS 398 forms that can be filled out using software such as Microsoft Word. There are many sources of "word processable" PHS 398 forms; these can be found by using the following terms for searching the Internet: "phs398" (or "phs 398") and "download." A note of caution—if you choose to download the PHS 398 from a non-NIH source, verify that it is the most up-to-date version and that it is complete and accurate.

Identify your audience. "Grantsmanship" is the equivalent of "scientific salesmanship." As with any type of sales, in order to be most effective, the presentation should be tailored for the intended audience. In this case, the audience will be a study section as well as an IC. As mentioned above, you can use the Web to identify the interests of the ICs as well as the expertise and the membership of the regularly constituted study sections.

Make your application a joy to read. The judgment of the study section is by far the most important factor in determining whether or not you will receive a grant, and the enthusiasm of the reviewers for your application is crucial to success. Thus, it is imperative that your application be not only scientifically sound, but enjoyable to read, as well. Consider that about a month prior to the study section meeting, each reviewer will receive a box of seventy to 100 applications, ten to twenty of which must be read thoroughly, critiqued, and learned well enough to be discussed knowledgeably in the face-to-face study section meeting. This means that, on average, a reviewer will have a maximum of only two to three days to devote to your particular application, and during that time the reviewer also may have to teach classes, write and grade exams, meet with students, solve problems in the lab, and attend committee meetings! It follows, therefore, that an application has the best chance of being successful if it is written clearly, logically, and succinctly, with the central points not obscured by mountains of detail. Include all of the background information required for your presentation to be understood; do not require that reviewers go to the library to look up the relevant references. Make their job as easy as possible.

"Hypothesis-driven" research sells well. It cannot be denied that an empirical, data-gathering approach has led to many significant scientific discoveries. Despite the historical importance of such "serendipity-driven" research, most of the proposals that are reviewed enthusiastically and result in funded NIH grants involve "hypothesis-driven" research. Some applications concern methods development research, but the best of these tend to be presented in the context of testing one or more hypotheses. In the "Specific Aims" section of the PHS 398, hypotheses should be identified, and the aims of the project should be stated clearly and succinctly. Often it is helpful to organize the "Research Design and Methods" section (see below) in terms of specific hypotheses and experimental tests, so that it parallels the "Specific Aims" section.

> *Most of the proposals that result in funded grants involve 'hypothesis-driven' research.*

Showcase both focus and vision. The specific aims should be realistic in the context of the time frame of the project, and formulated so as to address the central hypothesis in a logical and compelling manner. This is what is meant by "focus." "Vision" refers to the long-term direction of the project. If all goes well, how will the project develop? Where do you expect the project to be going in another five years? These questions need not be addressed directly under "Specific Aims," but it may be useful to provide your long-term view somewhere in the application, and the specific aims should be consistent with that vision.

Be scholarly. The "Specific Aims" section is followed by a "Background and Significance" section. While "Background and Significance" should not be an exhaustively detailed literature review, it should set the stage for your proposed project by describing, or at least referring to, all relevant prior studies and clearly summarizing the current status of the field. This section should be thoroughly documented with citations that lead to the original literature, not simply to review articles. Not only do you need to educate the readers, but you also need to convince them that you are knowledgeable about prior work in the area. It is natural for a reviewer to assume that the scholarship that you have shown in writing the background section (and other parts of the application, for that matter) is indicative of the thoroughness and insight that will attend the planning, execution, and interpretation of the proposed experiments.

Avoid an overly linear research plan. Generally, it is not wise to design your project so that each experiment is dependent on the success of the preceding experiment. What happens if one of the experiments fails or provides an inconclusive result? Present alternative approaches, and if possible, design your project so that you can investigate several hypotheses in parallel.

Include sufficient preliminary results for "proof of principle." The third section of the research plan is "Progress Report/Preliminary Studies." A number of years ago, it might have been sufficient to describe a few experiments from other labs in support of your own, well-documented research plan. However, there is now an expectation that preliminary results be provided to demonstrate the workability of any key steps in your project. The more linear the research plan, the more important it will be to have preliminary data.

Stress logic and rationale. Arguably the most important section of the application is "Research Design and Methods," since this is where you detail your plans for the proposed project period. Once again, you should strive for clarity in this section, showcasing the logic of your overall plan and the rationale for your proposed experiments. Some of the most successful applications break "Research Design and Methods" into subsections, in which each one presents a hypothesis or a question followed by an experiment or set of experiments that will provide a clear test of the hypothesis.

Identify potential weak points and ambiguities, and provide backup approaches when necessary. Every project includes speculative experiments, which could be quite exciting. However, your failure to acknowledge the potential weaknesses may be taken as evidence of poor judgment. When you do propose a risky approach, provide a backup plan in case of failure.

Anticipate experimental results and describe how you would interpret them. Generally, experienced PIs with extensive track records have an advantage in competing for research grants. This is because the judgment and productivity of the PI have already been demonstrated. One way that a new PI can establish credibility is to speculate about the possible outcomes of the proposed experiments, describe how each of these outcomes would be interpreted, and propose logical follow-up experiments. Nevertheless, in most cases this is not an adequate substitute for preliminary results, particularly in the case of an R01 application.

Provide a prioritized and realistic timetable. As mentioned above, it is important that your project be focused and realistic. One very effective way to demonstrate this is by prioritizing your goals and providing a timetable for the project. Most often, this will be presented at the end of the "Research Design and Methods" section.

Have zero tolerance for errors. Your application must be as error-free as possible. This is always important, but it is *absolutely critical* for a new PI, whose capabilities as a researcher and project director are unproven. If the application includes misspellings, poor grammar, uneven margins, and typographical errors, then why should one believe that the research would be accomplished any more carefully?

Prepare neat, legible graphics. Make sure that your graphics are large enough to be legible, even to individuals with less-than-perfect eyesight. Do your layout neatly and carefully. Avoid images whose quality would be degraded by repeated photocopying. If there are color or gray-scale graphics, make certain that photocopying of your application will not hurt their interpretability. Keep in mind that most of the study section members will receive photocopies of your proposal, not originals.

Submitting your application

Having investigated the relevant links on the NIH Web site and contacted the appropriate people at NIH, you should have a good idea of the IC(s) and study section(s) that would be most appropriate for your application. It is advisable to enclose a cover letter with your application, recommending specific IC and study section assignments. The choice of IC(s) will depend on the enthusiasm of program staff for the research area, and up to three NIH ICs may be listed, in order of preference. Up to three study section choices also may be specified.

In addition, the cover letter should briefly describe the research topic and the areas of technical expertise that will be required for a thorough review. Any potential conflicts of interest involving individual study section members or other scientists who might be recruited to serve as temporary reviewers for a single meeting of the study section should also be mentioned. Thus, you should list the names and affiliations of your competitors as well as any individuals with whom you have had differences or problems in the past and whom you suspect might not be able to judge your application impartially.

Receipt and referral of your application

There are two assignments made when an application is submitted to

NIH. The Division of Receipt and Referral in the Center for Scientific Review (CSR) will assign a new application both to a study section cluster, called an Integrated Review Group (IRG), and to an IC. As an example, chemistry-related research applications typically are assigned to the Medicinal Chemistry (MCHA) or Bioorganic and Natural Products (BNP) study sections, but they also will be assigned to an IC, such as NIGMS or the National Cancer Institute (NCI). Assignments for applications proposing research in other biomedical disciplines are handled in an analogous fashion. The CSR referral officer will consider seriously any assignment requests that are made in a cover letter that accompanies the application (see above); however, sometimes the Referral Officer will disagree and, with appropriate justification, will make another assignment.

Review process and review criteria

While funding is awarded only by the ICs, the review of most R01s and R15s is carried out by study sections in CSR. A typical study section will be a panel of about twenty reviewers with expertise and experience that is appropriate to the set of applications that will be reviewed. At the meeting, these reviewers will discuss applications assigned to a variety of ICs. The SRA recruits the reviewers for the panel and makes the review assignments for the applications. The two reviewers and reader assigned to each application will lead the discussion, which usually will last fifteen to thirty minutes. Obviously, the immediate impact of the research and the clarity of writing are extremely important! IC program staff usually attend these study section meetings to listen to the reviews. Subsequently, the program director (PD) to whom the application has been assigned may discuss the review with the applicant.

There are five review criteria for all research grants, including R01 and R15 applications. The criteria are *significance, approach, innovation, investigator, and environment.* In addition, AREA proposals from eligible institutions are evaluated on the characteristics of the student population, the likely impact of the award on the research environment, and the evidence that students at that institution have previously entered or are likely to enter careers in the biomedical and behavioral sciences.

It is up to the reviewers to determine how much weight each is given to each of the five review criteria. Sometimes reviewers will find sufficient strength in some criteria that weaknesses in other criteria may be forgiven. For example, a risky but very high impact proposal may be given an outstanding score despite the lack of preliminary data that might usually be expected. At other times, despite positive evaluation in most areas, including an outstanding PI with clear expertise, a sound approach, and a supportive environment, the reviewers will give a poor score because the research project may be derivative or incremental and therefore lacks significance and impact.

The following description of the review criteria is taken from material available on the NIH Web site and inserted here (with section heads *in italics*) for discussion and for educating potential applicants. For the purpose of illustration, each criterion is followed by the sort of positive and negative comments that may be heard from reviewers during actual study section meetings. These comments should be kept in mind during preparation of a grant application, in order to avoid common problems.

SIGNIFICANCE: Does this study address an important problem? If the aims of the application are achieved, how will scientific knowledge be advanced? What will be the effects of these studies on the concepts or methods that drive this field?
- This will have a huge impact and fill a big gap in the field.
- The potential benefit of new targets for understanding and treating these diseases is enormous.
- This is extremely important work that few people are doing but that needs to be done.
- Why didn't I think of this?
- Even if all the experiments work, no one will care or use the data.
- The results are only incremental extensions of what is already known.
- The results will generate very limited interest and not be applicable for other systems or organisms.
- The prior success in other laboratories diminishes the significance of this effort.

APPROACH: Are the conceptual framework, design, methods, and analyses adequately developed, well integrated, and appropriate to the aims of the project? Does the applicant acknowledge potential problem areas and consider alternative tactics?
- A pleasure to read because the PI considered the possible results, their interpretation, the potential weaknesses of the approach, and other independent methods to test the hypothesis.
- Well thought-out and well written.

147

- The PI takes a highly mechanistic approach toward analyzing these reactions, thereby providing a framework upon which future discoveries and applications will emerge.
- Proof of principle has already been demonstrated.
- The experiments proposed are clearly presented, logical, and demonstrate considerable creativity.
- Experiments do not directly or appropriately test the hypothesis.
- The experiments are hard to follow.
- More preliminary data showing the feasibility of the approach would improve this aim.
- It is not clear what new insight will be gained about possible mechanisms.
- The "Approach" section reads like a list of methods with too many irrelevant details.
- The results will be indirect or descriptive.
- There is an overreliance on a single method.
- This aim does not fit in with the other aims.
- There are major concerns that the aims will not be accomplished using this approach.
- This proposal deals with very complex, interdependent systems. Thus, while the application was insightful, the approaches are frequently tedious and difficult to follow.
- The proposal is strong on theory and speculation, but somewhat less impressive on supporting evidence.
- This application is overly ambitious, with too many experiments for the proposed project period.
- The PI should have included a stronger rationale for these experiments.
- The PI does not indicate how data gained from these experiments would be interpreted.
- These studies are not worth the time relative to the amount of information they will produce.

INNOVATION: Does the project employ novel concepts, approaches or methods? Are the aims original and innovative? Does the project challenge existing paradigms or develop new methodologies or technologies?
- The PI will develop new approaches to answer previously unanswerable questions.

- This is a novel mechanism that has the potential to explain previously perplexing results.
- This is a crazy idea that just might work.
- These new or modified methods will have wide application and impact.
- Exceptional opportunities for innovation characterize a well-organized and polished presentation.
- The methods are standard, but the questions asked are novel and the results will have wide impact.
- The results are derivative and would corroborate what is already known.
- These questions and approaches have been asked and used by other laboratories.

INVESTIGATOR: Is the investigator appropriately trained and well suited to carry out this work? Is the work appropriate to the experience level of the principal investigator and other researchers (if any)?

- The PI has a strong record of research productivity in the field.
- Careful, rigorous, and exciting research is a hallmark of this PI.
- The PI has supervised several undergraduates in the last few years and should be an excellent mentor.
- The collaborators have had a long-standing research relationship with the PI.
- The expertise of the collaborators is complementary to that of the investigator.
- Productivity has been very low in the past several years and there is no indication that this will change.
- The investigator or collaborator does not have the expertise required for the proposed research.
- The PI seems to lack the background, experience and perspective required to succeed on this project.
- The PI's postdoctoral experience is good preparation for the proposed studies; however, one publication as an independent PI in four years makes it difficult to assess his potential.
- There are no letters from the listed collaborators.
- There are letters but little information about collaborators' roles.
- The collaborator is very busy so it is not clear what the commitment is to the proposed research.

ENVIRONMENT: Does the scientific environment in which the work will be done contribute to the probability of success? Do the proposed experiments take advantage of unique features of the scientific environment or employ useful collaborative arrangements? Is there evidence of institutional support?

- The institution has provided all the resources necessary for the PI to succeed.
- The PI's limited expertise is balanced by the availability of the institution's resource center and its director.
- Institutional support is provided through a reduced teaching load for the PI and through equipment purchase.
- Resources at the home institution are limited, but the PI has arranged to use facilities at other institutions and at a nearby company.
- The past record of good student interest in research and the availability of qualified collaborators bode well for the success of this AREA grant application.
- The institution has an exceptional record for educating students going on to Ph.D. or M.D. degrees.
- The PI has limited access to the required equipment so there are concerns about potential productivity.
- The existing computer is not suitable to run up-to-date programs and to compute the proposed structures.
- The contribution of institutional support is extremely vague and should be clarified.
- The PI has not taken advantage of potential collaborators available in the same institution.
- The research environment does not seem to be very supportive.

Review and scoring

Although CSR's chartered study sections review mostly R01 grant applications, they also review applications for other types of grants, including R15s. AREA proposals are usually reviewed in a cluster apart from the review of R01s at the same study section meeting. If there is a large number of AREA applications, they may also be reviewed by a temporary study section known as a Special Emphasis Panel.

Following the discussion of each application, the study section members vote to assign a priority score. The priority score, which reflects the perceived quality of the proposed science, is between 100 and 500. The "outstanding" scores are usually in the low to mid-100s, whereas the "acceptable" scores usually range from 300 to 500. NIH presently does not usually assign priority scores for R01 applications considered to be in the lower half of all the applications under consideration, so an application that might otherwise receive a score of 300 or higher is not discussed and is designated "unscored." This practice is known as "streamlining." The recommendation to streamline an application is made by the assigned reviewers before the review meeting and finalized at the beginning of the meeting. If any member of the study section disagrees with the "unscored" designation, the application will be discussed and scored after all. Many of these will receive scores worse than 300. After the meeting, the actual score assigned by each reviewer to each proposal (as well as the "unscored" designation, when appropriate) is entered into the NIH computer system, which calculates an overall priority score. The priority scores for all of the applications are normalized by percentiling according to past and present study section scoring behavior. This prevents study sections from unjustly rewarding or penalizing applicants by systematically lenient or harsh scoring, respectively, and ensures that a certain percentage of proposals from each study section will receive scores that will make them eligible for funding.

R15 and other special program applications are given scores according to the merit of the proposed research and how well they fit the criteria of the special program. R15 proposals, however, are not percentiled; instead, funding decisions are based on the priority scores as well as the content of the summary statements. This is because some study sections review so few R15s that percentile rankings would not be statistically meaningful. To use the R01 scores as a basis for percentiling would be equally inappropriate, since these two funding mechanisms are not directly comparable.

Revision and resubmission

If the initial proposal does not receive a fundable score or if it is unscored, the PI has up to two more chances to revise and resubmit the application. This should not be done hastily, but only after careful consideration of the comments in the summary statement. Often it is useful to consult with colleagues or the NIH program director, who may be able to help with the interpretation of comments in the summary statement. How effectively the applicant responds to the critiques is extremely important, since the critiques are made available to the next group of reviewers. The PI should take full advantage of the additional three-page "Introduction" section permitted in an amended application to respond to each criticism, either justifying the original research plan or describing modifications to the proposal. It is important to respond thoughtfully to the reviewers' concerns. If the original criticism was "off base," then a cogent explanation in the "Introduction" should be provided to the reviewers of the revised application. Any significant changes to the application should be indicated clearly, as a courtesy to the reviewers. A particularly effective way of indicating changes is to draw a vertical bar in the margin alongside modified sections.

Funding

The PD will make recommendations on funding to the institute director, based on the availability of funds, the research priorities of the IC, and the percentiles and priority scores. Funding for R01 grants comes from the ICs, but the funds for the AREA program are provided by the Office of the Director, NIH. AREA applications from all of the ICs are ranked by priority score, and the number of proposals that are funded depends upon the dollars available for that fiscal year. After the total number of potential awards has been calculated, the number of proposals from each IC that could be funded is added up. Depending on the number of proposals with fundable scores from each IC, the funds are dispersed to the various ICs for their final funding decisions. For example, NIGMS, which recently has funded between 20 to 30 percent of the R15 grants, may have ten to fifteen slots in each of the three review-funding cycles in a year. The Institute may elect to fund all of these proposals in rank order, but it could also decide to fund out of order because of the Institute's priorities in specific research areas. Some ICs will even fund a few AREA proposals with their own funds, in order to extend the number of awards to well-deserving PIs with meritorious research projects.

Conclusion

The purpose of this chapter has been twofold: to provide practical information regarding the relevant research grant funding mechanisms that are available through NIH, the processes of NIH peer review and funding, and sources of additional information; and also to show that it is possible, and there is ample precedent, for faculty from less research-intensive colleges and universities to obtain NIH funding for research.

In a funding competition in which slight differences in percentile rankings or priority scores are crucial, every aspect of the grant application must be as strong as possible. *Especially* in cases where the sponsoring institution is a less research-intensive school, the research environment and the quality of the school's commitment to scientific research can be critical.

One of the most important messages that we wish to impart is that there are many people who can provide useful information and advice to a grant applicant. These include administrators at the PI's school, faculty colleagues, scientific collaborators, and NIH personnel. NIH funding is highly competitive, and whether a PI chooses to prepare an application in isolation or with ample input and feedback from these individuals can spell the *You have to play in order to win.* difference between failure and success in landing an NIH grant.

Finally, there has never been an NIH research grant awarded for which an application has not been submitted. You have to play in order to win. *No deposit, no return.* Æ

TABLE IV
Useful NIH Web Sites

Starting points with many links

NIGMS Funding Links:
  http://www.nigms.nih.gov/funding/funding.html

Links Concerning Extramural Programs at NIH Institutes
  http://grants.nih.gov/grants/policy/emprograms/index.html

THE APPLICATION PROCESS

  The NIH Homepage:
    http://www.nih.gov

  Answers to Frequently Asked Questions about NIH Grants:
    http://grants.nih.gov/grants/funding/giofaq.htm

  Twenty-five Helpful Hints for New Investigators from NIGMS Staff:
    http://www.nigms.nih.gov/funding/tips.html

  Application Receipt, Referral and Review,
    Center for Scientific Review:
      http://grants.nih.gov/grants/funding/submissionschedule.htm
      http://www.csr.nih.gov/

  NIH Grant Application (PHS 398) Instructions/
    Guidelines and Forms:
      http://grants.nih.gov/grants/forms.htm

  NIH Modular Grant Information, Q&A,
    Sample Budget and Biosketch:
      http://grants.nih.gov/grants/funding/modular/modular.htm

THE REVIEW PROCESS

  The Five Review Criteria for Most NIH Applications:
    http://grants.nih.gov/grants/guide/notice-files/not97-010.html

  Descriptions of Integrated Review Groups at the
    Center for Scientific Review:
      http://www.csr.nih.gov/review/irgdesc.htm

  NIH Center for Scientific Review Study Section Rosters:
    http://www.csr.nih.gov/committees/rosterindex.asp

THE FUNDING COMPONENTS OF NIH

Home Pages of the NIH Institutes, Centers, and Offices:
http://www.nih.gov/icd/

NIH GUIDE FOR GRANTS AND CONTRACTS

Program Announcements (PAs) and
Request for Applications (RFAs), *inter alia*:
http://grants.nih.gov/grants/guide/index.html

DATA ON ACTIVE GRANTS

CRISP Database for NIH-Funded Research Projects:
http://commons.cit.nih.gov/crisp/owa/CRISP.Generate_Ticket

SPECIAL PROGRAMS AT NIH

AREA or R15 for Non-Research Intensive Colleges
and Universities:
http://grants.nih.gov/grants/funding/area.htm

NIGMS Division of Minority Opportunities in Research:
http://www.nigms.nih.gov/about_nigms/more.html

THERE IS TRAGEDY IN THE WAVE of building construction that is taking place in many of this nation's liberal arts colleges. The architectural designs, classrooms, and laboratories are attractive, but they are only a shell to cover what should be going on inside. Without the tools of modern science, new buildings are merely the wrapping for an ordinary experience.

(Photo: An undergraduate research lab at Hendrix College.)

Michael P. Doyle is Vice President of Research Corporation.

MICHAEL P. DOYLE

10 THE COST OF RESEARCH INSTRUMENTATION IN CHEMISTRY

WHEN ASKED WHY THEY THOUGHT research in chemistry was too expensive, a group of college administrators responded that the financial resources to acquire and maintain "research instrumentation" were beyond their means. "How can I be fair with my faculty," asked one college president, "when my chemists ask for $50,000 in matching funds for new instruments, the chair of my music department wants $20,000 for new pianos, my director for instructional services says we need a new computer facility—to mention only a few requests—and I can only allocate $150,000 for capital expenditures this year." He answered, only half inquisitively, "Isn't it better to allocate a fractional amount to each department?" "Or better yet," a provost from a liberal arts college offered to the group, "why not set up an internal system for evaluation of requests with faculty representatives who have responsibility to prioritize individual and departmental proposals?" The conversation continued with a general acknowledgment that in any system of cost allocation, research had to have the lower priority. "Research is too expensive" is an answer that is often given without adequate cost analysis. However, as will be related here, *a first-class operation for basic research in the chemical sciences can be set up and maintained at such a reasonable cost that most undergraduate institutions can afford to be centers of excellence.*

The questions asked by the group of administrators cannot be answered adequately without addressing the importance of research in undergraduate education. Although this has been done in earlier chapters, it is perhaps useful to reiterate that only institutions with strong science programs which educate students who can address societal problems will be *centers of excellence,* and the basis of strong science programs is encouragement and facilitation of research with undergraduate students.

The basic set

Ask any knowledgeable collection of chemists or the American Chemical Society's Committee on Professional Training "what is the set of instruments most characteristic of institutions that promote research and education?" and the response will be—

Nuclear Magnetic Resonance (NMR) Spectrometer
Mass Spectrometer (MS)
Infrared (IR) Spectrometer
Atomic Absorption (AA) Spectrometer
Gas Chromatograph (GC) with Integrator
High Pressure Liquid Chromatograph (HPLC)
Ultraviolet/visible (UV/vis) spectrophotometer
Small equipment

—the last entry referring to items like analytical balances, pH meters, computers, and selective ion monitors whose unit costs are only a fraction of a spectrometer or chromatograph. Without explaining the specific function of each instrument, spectrometers provide information about molecular structure whereas chromatographs measure amounts and purity. All are considered to be essential to a quality education in the chemical sciences.

Arguments can be made for what is not included in the list—a centrifuge or electrophoresis setup for biochemical investigations, electrochemical equipment, for example—and some would argue that atomic absorption spectroscopy is not necessary or that capillary electrophoresis has replaced HPLC. In these cases, replace those items on the list with the instrument that you find more viable. What does remain clear, however, is that the NMR, MS, IR, and UV/vis spectrometers, and the GC, are essential to all chemistry department programs in teaching and in research; the atomic absorption spectrometer or the HPLC may be exchanged for spectroscopic or separations instrumentation more appropriate to the program or to faculty interests.

The research of the synthetic chemist is the most instrument-intensive, and an able practitioner requires most of the items on the instrument list for routine separations and analyses. For these chemists viable research and education programs require routine hands-on access to NMR, IR, MS, and chromatography instrumentation, and the proximal distance to reach the instrumentation is important. In other words, *this instrumentation cannot be at another institution, even if across the street, or housed in a building on the other side of campus and still be considered accessible.* Proximal distance is important, not only for reasons akin to having a library close to faculty offices, but also for control of maintenance, sample delivery, and, especially, overall use and access.

For the analytical chemist a capillary electrophoresis set-up might

TABLE 1

Cost for acquisition and maintenance of chemistry instrumentation

Instrument	Capital Unit Cost ($K)	Annual Cost ($K) for Maintenance
NMR (300 MHz)	$200	$ 4
MS (ion selective monitor)	60	<1
IR (FT-IR, ± 2 cm^{-1})	30	<1
UV/vis (diode array)	16	<1
GC/integrator (2 column capillary)	24	<1
HPLC (dual pump) with data station	25	<1
AA (standard furnace)	35	<1
Miscellaneous	50	≤1
Total	$440	<$10

be desirable, and a physical chemist may require laser systems. The computational chemist has pressing need for a high-end computer, and a materials chemist might require a differential scanning calorimeter. In all of these cases the need, if justified, can be met. Faculty at undergraduate institutions have, for a long time, justified instruments such as these in proposals submitted to private and public funding agencies for research and education.

So, if this kind of instrumentation constitutes what is needed to achieve excellence, what is the cost? The answer is given in the sum of the costs for the selection of specified instruments in Table 1.

The capital costs are realistic and, in some cases, are somewhat excessive estimates, rather than being based on the bargain-basement deals available to an elite few. The annual costs for maintenance include all supplies, including chromatography columns (two per year), liquid nitrogen and liquid helium, and paper; repair costs are not included since this variable is not predictable, but estimates of percent of the purchase cost of "large-ticket" items such as NMR are realistic.

According to the 1995 CUR Directory for Chemistry Departments, more than 120 predominantly undergraduate institutions were in possession of a high-field NMR spectrometer. Today more than 250 have high-field NMR instrumentation.

If the average lifetime of major instruments can be estimated to be ten years, then the annualized cost of the instruments listed in Table 1 is approximately $50,000. In other words, *a high-quality set of chemical instruments can be acquired and maintained for the tuition cost of fewer than three students at most private colleges, or for less than 0.5% of student tuition at a 10,000-student public institution.* More than four times these costs are required by small liberal arts colleges each year just to support their administrative information systems.

Teaching instrument or research instrument?

Some faculty would argue that they can obtain four teaching instruments for the price of one $24,000 GC/integrator. The teaching instrument is "adequate" if you only have $6,000 to spend, but the same instrument will usually be inadequate as a research instrument. Furthermore, the $24,000 instrument may provide a throughput of samples greater than four times that of the $6,000 instrument, meaning, of course, that the output from 4 x $6,000 is much less than that from 1 x $24,000. The same can be said of other instruments: *beware of low-cost alternatives to research-grade instruments.*

Just as sample throughput is a criterion for instrument efficiency, so student throughput is a determinant of institutional efficiency which is a measure of quality. The larger the number of students, the greater the number of instruments required for the laboratory. Thus if one instrument is able to handle ten students' samples per hour, then, ideally, thirty students can have their samples processed during one three-hour laboratory. However, with forty students in the laboratory and only one instrument, ten students go wanting for sample analysis. In this latter case, either the instructor must increase sample throughput per unit time, usually by changing the experiment, or a second instrument is required.

"Well, if all that is necessary to change the number of required instruments is to change the experiment, why does anyone need more than one instrument?" asked one college administrator. "Faculty should be able to modify all experiments to deliver minimum cost per experiment." This argument belies cost/benefit considerations and erodes quality as a measure of excellence. Would you advise the music department to use only one piano for all of the students wishing to practice even when that means only five minutes of exposure to the instrument per student?

The $440,000 capital investment in chemistry instrumentation does not insure excellence. What faculty and students do with this investment is the measure of excellence. There are numerous schools that have this instrumentation, and it receives limited use during most of the year; others employ the investment productively, as measured by student use, faculty publications, and research grant support. In this latter case, *students are enriched, faculty participate in their field's evolution, and the reputation of the institution is enhanced.* When this instrumentation is not available, the quality of education is lower, the power to attract capable faculty is diminished, and the ability of the institution's graduates to reach their full potential is restricted.

If the investment of $440,000 in instrumentation for chemistry is a first level of preparedness, what will more than $2 million in capital investment bring? The answer is Furman University (Chapter 8)! An independent, private liberal arts college in Greenville, South Carolina with approximately 3,000 undergraduate students, Furman boasts a chemistry department with nine faculty that graduates more than thirty majors each year. In 1996 this institution became the first predominantly undergraduate institution to have a 500 MHz NMR spectrometer (in addition to their 300 MHz instrument). Their holdings of instruments are second to none in broad categories (see page 126). Their productivity, by all measures of achievement, is exceptional. Thirty years ago this institution was a quality regional university; now Furman University has national standing.

The same could be said of Hope College, an institution of comparable size to Furman University and located in Holland, Michigan, amid tulips and an authentic Dutch windmill. Hope was one of the first undergraduate institutions to obtain an NMR spectrometer (1967; see Chapter 11) and earnestly sought to continue to obtain research-grade instruments. Proposals submitted to federal agencies requesting a mass spectrometer were returned, however, often with the comment "this instrument doesn't belong in an undergraduate institution." Assembling nearly $20,000 in discretionary funds and relying on alumni for assistance, the department of chemistry purchased a slightly used system in the mid-1970s. Not surprisingly, proposals submitted for *Funding comes to those who invest in themselves.* funding of major instruments in subsequent years, often at a rate of more than one per year, were funded with regularity. Perhaps there is a lesson here: *funding comes to those who invest in themselves.*

Matching support for instrumentation

Science, and especially the chemical sciences, holds a special place among academic disciplines in being able to attract matching support for instrumentation. This is based mainly on research potential, but also on innovation in education. Gone are the days when the Pew Charitable Trusts accepted what was basically a shopping list from college presidents for $200,000 outlays of equipment for science. What we have instead is a complex array of public and private sources that fund requests for instruments. These requests have a high potential for success when the criteria for awards are well understood, but this is the subject for another chapter.

Most college administrators have limited understanding of the processes required for instrument acquisition, and few have a rational plan that can be understood within institutional objectives. Some rely on others for advice regarding the appropriateness of an expensive instrument for their institution, and a few object to acquisitions that are not equalized among all departments. However, there are guiding principles that can be used to effectively measure need and benefit:

- Is this an instrument that will be used extensively in research and teaching?
- What is the projected use of the instrument in number of hours per week?
- Is this instrument of critical importance to the professionalism of one or more faculty?
- Should this instrument be proposed and acquired as a departmental instrument or one for a smaller faculty unit?
- What is the probability that external funding can be obtained to cover one-half or more of the capital cost for this instrument?
- Will the acquisition of this instrument require building renovation?
- What are the projected annual costs for maintenance and supplies?
- If breakdown occurs, who will repair the instrument, and what will it cost?
- Who will take responsibility for instructing the users, obtaining routine supplies, and performing maintenance?

The bottom line is that the capital outlays for research instruments are not the only costs associated with their acquisition. Faculty must be willing to invest their time and efforts in writing proposals, using

the instruments productively, and maintaining the instruments for op-
timum operations. The faculty that take advantage of these opportunities enrich themselves, their students, and their institution which
becomes a center of excellence.

A recent campus visit brought me to an institution that was in the
final stages of completing a new science building. The classrooms were
elegant and fitted with modern audio/visual
capabilities. The laboratories were spacious
with fume hoods in chemistry laboratories
that offered safe exposure to a multitude of
chemicals. Most faculty would love to be
housed in such facilities, and students would
be drawn to science by the quality of the
classrooms and labs. However, even in a brief
visit, one could notice that there were few

> The National Science Foundation's
> Directorate for Mathematics and
> Physical Sciences received only
> 148 RUI proposals in 1988,
> but funded 50. There were
> 146 RUI proposals in 1997,
> and 71 were funded.

modern instruments held by the science departments. And when I
asked the faculty, "where are your modern instruments?" I was informed that they had very few. No high-field NMR, no GC/MS, no FT-
IR, but the cost of the building was greater than $30 million!

Not only had no allocation been made for instrumentation to be
included in the new building, but there was a moratorium on expendi-
tures for instruments. When I asked a new faculty member in the
chemistry department, "Have you written a proposal to request funds
for a high-field NMR spectrometer?" this untenured assistant professor
answered, "We can't write the proposal because the institution refuses
to offer matching costs." A visit to the dean brought this answer to my
inquiry: "Don't you think our investment of more than $30 million
demonstrates sufficient dedication to science that foundations will
overlook the absence of instruments and, in fact, be more willing to
pay the full costs of these acquisitions?" The answer, of course, is "no."

There is tragedy in the wave of building construction that is taking
place in many of this nation's liberal arts colleges. The architectural
designs, classrooms, and laboratories are attractive, but they are only
a shell to cover what should be going on inside. Without the tools of
modern science, new buildings are merely the wrapping for an ordinary experience. Æ

I'T'S HARD TO SAY HOW LONG it would have taken Hope to convince National Science Foundation of its worthiness for its own NMR spectrometer. It would have happened eventually. But we probably would have waited in a line with many other really fine liberal arts colleges. As it was, our acquisition of a "major instrument" was almost more important than the specific instrument itself.

(Above: 1967 photo of Douglas C. Neckers at Hope College.)

Douglas C. Neckers is Director of the Center for Photochemical Sciences at Bowling Green State University.

DOUGLAS C. NECKERS

11 THE FIRST NMR SPECTROMETER AT HOPE

BY 1966 OR SO IT BECAME INCREASINGLY clear that nuclear magnetic resonance spectroscopy was central to research in organic chemistry. Thus, I decided that Hope needed an NMR spectrometer. I'm not sure my colleagues shared my enthusiasm, but President Calvin VanderWerf was well aware of the technique, and he also thought we needed such instrumentation. Enthusiasm from Cal meant it was my job to raise most of the money for the spectrometer. When the time came, he'd be there to provide enthusiastic moral support and help in convincing donors I had identified to provide the final dollars.

I was driven by the task of getting an NMR for Hope, since this too would prove our parity with university colleagues. So I set about the task with gusto. As I recall, I wrote at least one proposal to the NSF and got the typical response. "You're in a four-year school. We've got research universities to take care of." (That wasn't entirely the case. Some small schools did get funding for major instruments. At the time, I think NSF funded one NMR spectrometer per year in a non-Ph.D. granting institution.) But after banging on NSF's door once, I decided there had to be a better way. So I used another principle I had learned early in the 1950s *Never send troops through the middle of the opponent's army when you can go around the end.* as an undergraduate student at a school which required that every freshman be enrolled in the Reserve Officers Training Corps (ROTC). One of the principles of being a good general, some crusty sergeant taught us, was never send troops through the middle of the opponent's army when you can go around the end.

Base funding

Public universities were growing almost uncontrollably, and the federal government was trying to assist the states in providing facilities to help them cope with enormous growth. At about this time the U.S. Department of Education came into existence and developed a series of grants and initiatives to help universities with their burgeoning enrollments. Hope's treasurer told me of a report he received that highlighted opportunities for institutions to share in various governmental programs.

NUCLEAR MAGNETIC RESONANCE

When physicists Felix Bloch at Stanford University and, separately, Edward M. Purcell at Harvard and their respective collaborators discovered nuclear magnetic resonance in 1946, they had no inkling that this technique would be used for medical imaging. . . . It was known from quantum mechanics, and it had been experimentally demonstrated by Otto Stern and Isador Rabi . . . that certain atomic nuclei, including hydrogen, have a magnetic moment. That is to say that these nuclei act like tiny magnets and, like magnets in a strong magnetic field, the majority of them will line up with the field. This, in turn, was demonstrated by the absorption and resulting resonance of radio frequency radiation, hence the name "nuclear magnetic resonance."

Chemists soon discovered the usefulness of NMR. They found that the resonance frequency of the nuclei of hydrogen (and, later, of the heavy isotope of carbon) depends on their chemical environment: Different substances show different resonance frequencies. Since carbon and hydrogen are the principal ingredients of organic molecules . . . it comes as no surprise that NMR instruments are found in all major chemical laboratories!

—*Science and Serendipity,* Ernest L. Eliel, 1992[1]

He knew that I was seeking funding for a BIG instrument and helped me identify a program of funding administered by the state which provided matching funds for instructional equipment at colleges and universities.

The one catch in the program was that funding was enrollment-based. In order to justify getting funds, the applicant had to demonstrate that the equipment would benefit a *large*, growing number of students. "Large, growing" in this instance meant "hoards and hoards" of students, (i.e., mass education). The problem was that Hope's enrollment was barely holding even.

This may be the one of the few times in the history of education that an NMR spectrometer was described as if it were a slide projector in a classroom serving thousands of undergraduates in a school the size of Michigan State. I don't think I counted any dead bodies in determining undergraduate enrollments to benefit from this marvelous new technique, but I counted every live one I could muster. Among chemistry students I counted all the research students, every undergraduate taking organic, all of the summer institute high school teachers, and probably a janitor and a stockroom keeper. In order to improve Hope's figures, I also added a large number of mechanical calculators to the proposal and got the math department to set up a stand-alone calculator (!) laboratory for all freshmen students who took mathematics. (Computers existed then, but Hope had no computer science program and almost no one had used a computer except a few physicists and chemists.) The director of development and I drove my offering to Lansing a few days before the July deadline.

Matching funds

In a relatively short time, I found out that my effort had been successful; some government agency, either federal or state, would give us the bucks if we met the matching requirements. The grant came with a commitment on the part of the institution to find a matching equivalent number of dollars. My right-wing campus colleagues were happy to point out that therein lies the fallacy (sin?) in accepting federal money; it always costs you more than you get. But accept the money we did—and with absolute glee—for with it Hope was within reaching distance of its first very own major instrument—an NMR spectrometer.

It wasn't as hard as it first seemed to find the matching funds to which I had committed the institution.

It wasn't as hard as it first seemed to find the matching funds to which I had committed the institution. Two chemical companies had manufacturing or process development facilities in Holland. Holland Color and Chemical, later BASF, made dyes. Parke Davis had their process development facility in Holland, and manufactured pharmaceuticals including chloromycetin. Though there was no research worthy of the name at either, there were scientists in the neighborhood and I thought they should be interested in helping Hope buy the NMR. I went off to find anyone I could at their respective facilities to tell them about the virtues of nuclear magnetic resonance spectroscopy.

Holland Color and Chemical's headquarters was located away from the manufacturing site on the south side of town, so I went to see a chemist there, and he introduced me to his manager. The manager told me the name of the president of the company and I recognized that he was an old friend of my family's from western New York. Thus armed I managed an appointment with him and the director of research, Frank Moser, a Hope undergraduate who had gotten his Ph.D. with Werner Bachmann at Michigan in the '30s and developed a fine reputation in phthalocyanine chemistry. Frank was a loyal alumnus and anxious to do what he could for his alma mater. I told Cal that I thought we actually could approach Holland Color and Chemical about some matching funds for the NMR. I know he thought this was not much of an idea, but he agreed to at least meet with their representatives if I could get them to come to his office. So I proceeded to get Frank, and the president of Holland Color and Chemical, which by this time had become a division of Chemtron, to do just that. After some preliminary chit-chat, Cal almost knocked me off my chair by asking my Chemtron friends to provide all the matching funds for the NMR spectrometer with a grant to the college. Since this amounted to about $18,000, I thought he would never get this amount of money, but offered, as my part of the bargain, that if they gave us the matching money, I would teach an organic qualitative analysis course at night for local industrial personnel. I'd teach them how to run spectra on their own samples, and help them in using the technique in their own work.

Never ask for too little. Always ask for too much. You might be surprised at the outcome.

A few weeks later, much to everyone's surprise, Cal received a letter stating that Chemtron would commit to a major grant for a large percentage of the matching money for the NMR! Cal feigned he was not surprised, but I was shocked. Worse yet, the funds for the NMR were now assembled, and we had to order the instrument. I was obligated to teach an organic course at night during the next semester, but that was a small price to pay for such an important major instrument. From this experience, however, I learned another lesson about fund raising. Never ask for too little. Always ask for too much. You might be surprised at the outcome.

Allocation of resources

Across campus my name became mud. "THE NMR" added fuel to the gossips' fire that under "this scientist president" the institution was heading down a fast track to hell. In the Kaffe Kletz, where campus philosophers went to smoke their pipes and offer their latest views on how the place should really be run, the wags were particularly abrasive. "When salaries for theologians, philosophers, political scientists and historians are so meager, the scientists are spending seven Cadillacs' worth of funding on a new research toy for Neckers? Why doesn't the president find funds from all those chemical companies he knows so well to increase our pay?" Of course, chemical companies at the time were in little need of philosophers, theologians, political scientists and general know-it-alls, so their pleas would have fallen on the deafest of ears even had they been uttered. But no matter. My NMR was taking bread out of their babies' mouths.

I don't recall much about the details involved in ordering the instrument but do recall spending sleepless nights over what I had gotten the institution into. In my little home town in western New York, one was really rich if one owned a Cadillac. I had managed to commit Hope College to buying an instrument that was roughly valued at the equivalent of seven Cadillacs! And for what? Undergraduate research? How could that be justified? Nevertheless, after I had researched all the available vendors carefully, we sent the order off to Varian Associates in the amount of $36,000 and a few cents.

Delivery

Sometime late in the winter I got a call from the Varian salesman saying that our NMR had been shipped from California, and that we could expect a call from the shipper with an approximate delivery time. The California office, however, slipped up, and the instrument arrived on our doorstep with no warning. I remember Irwin Brink appearing in my classroom to tell me the NMR had arrived in a moving van at the front door of the science hall. "The driver says that if we don't arrange to get that load off his truck in an hour, he'll take it back to California." Since the magnet weighed 1500 pounds, this was no idle threat and we had to come up with a plan in a hurry.

Fortunately, the person who was in charge of all campus operations, Henry Boersma, came to our rescue. He told us that a contractor building a new dormitory across the street from the science building, had a front-loading tractor on site. Henry was sure that front loader could get a heavy object off the truck. After some minor negotiations (can't imagine how this would have worked today with the various liabilities of all parties to contend with) the front loader pulled up to the rear of the truck, inserted its fork under my precious NMR magnet and managed to easily lift it off. Since Hope had no heavy-equipment-handling facilities on campus, we then faced the problem of what to do next. After all, an NMR magnet sitting on a front loader in the middle of Tenth Street in Holland, Michigan was not good for much even if it was "off the truck."

Once again Henry came to the rescue. Hope, at the time, owned three vehicles—the president's automobile, an early-'50s-vintage two-ton truck, and a jeep. The all-purpose truck was by far the most valuable. Though it hauled everything all over campus most of the year, it assumed a position of real importance when it hauled the football team to its practices and games. Using the truck for something like an NMR, however, was well beyond its abilities. The jeep was used mainly to plow snow in the winter, and it had an elevator lift on the back. As it turned out, this lift was strong enough to hold the magnet. So, it was to the jeep that we turned.

Hope's jeep was under the careful watch of Jim, the janitor. Without my intervention, or even approval, the NMR magnet was off-loaded onto the lift of Jim's ancient jeep. I could barely watch. The last recollection I have of the occasion was watching the most delicate part of my long-labored-for NMR being driven to the garage of a house the college had recently purchased across from the administration building. I can still see my NMR magnet flying through the February snow and remember wondering if it would manage to stay on the back of the jeep, and how it would survive its first cold winter day all alone in a garage. Since the garage was located at the top of a steep incline I could also imagine seven Cadillacs rolling off the back of the jeep down onto the snow of Twelfth Street as Jim glibly drove his jitney up the ramp to its regular home.

Jim was one of those really nice guys most campuses find indispensable. Since I worked odd hours in the science building, he would occasionally stop by when he was plowing campus walks, to warm up and chat. I remembered, from one of many visits with him, that Jim said he always had breakfast at a local diner, affectionately named after its owner—Horsethief Steve's. So at 5:00 a.m. the next morning I gave up on sleep, ventured out into the cold and accosted Jim at the counter of the diner.

"Where's my NMR magnet, Jim?" I asked.

"On the back of my jeep. It ain't goin' nowhere. Go home and go back to bed."

Fortunately Jim was right. A few hours later some heavy-equipment handlers arrived from Zeeland. Jim backed the jeep up to the front door of the science building, the equipment haulers wrestled the magnet off the back and rolled it on steel pipes down the first floor hall into the former girl's bathroom that had been reincarnated as "the NMR room." A couple of weeks later the installer arrived with the salesman to begin the installation. It was his first A-60 NMR installation and it took him about two weeks—which had to be some sort of record—but eventually he got us up and running. The Varian salesman bid farewell after the first day by announcing he was leaving the company. "I'm going to work for a new company in Massachusetts called Digital that makes computers. Suggest you buy some stock." If only I had followed his advice.

Once *the* NMR was installed, and I knew how to operate it myself, I tentatively began to incorporate NMR experiments into the undergraduate organic laboratory. This was a bit of a hassle, but we demonstrated the technique for at least some of the students who professed a modicum of interest. Some of the premeds were pretty skeptical. "What do I need an NMR for? I want to be a *real* doctor."

"What do I need an NMR for? I want to be a real doctor."

Ironically, today when I see these former students, mostly the proctologists, they quickly point out that NMR is about the only thing I taught them they still use. The technique is not the same nor is the name; they now call it Magnetic Resonance Imaging, (MRI) but recognize that they use NMR on a routine basis.

As far as my own research was concerned, the only real project *my* NMR helped was one that an undergraduate student, Jan Dopper, and I worked on a year or so before I left Hope. Jan who is now a member of the management committee of Akzo Organon, was another first—the first full-time research student ever to work in the labs at Hope.

It's hard to say how long it would have taken Hope to convince NSF of its worthiness for its own NMR spectrometer. It would have happened eventually. But we probably would have waited in a line with many other really fine liberal arts colleges. As it was, our acquisition of a major instrument was almost more important than the specific instrument itself. It demonstrated to the institution, and to an extent to undergraduate institutions more generally, that they could get into the instrument generation if they put their mind to it. With that came the recognition that their faculty could develop research careers as readily as their university counterparts. Æ

In 1977, Hope College was the first liberal arts college to receive NSF funding for the purchase of a Fourier-transform NMR spectrometer.

S INCE ITS BEGINNING, the Petroleum Research Fund has considered support of research at undergraduate institutions to be of special significance. When the first ACS-PRF advisory committee began looking at ways to use the PRF income, the importance of having undergraduate students involved in research was recognized. Since today's undergraduates become tomorrow's graduate students, faculty members and industrial researchers, providing research opportunities early in their scientific careers was considered extremely beneficial.

Lawrence A. Funke is Program Director of the American Chemical Society Petroleum Research Fund.

LAWRENCE A. FUNKE

12 ORIGIN AND PROGRAMS OF THE PETROLEUM RESEARCH FUND

THE PETROLEUM RESEARCH FUND (PRF), administered by the American Chemical Society (ACS), is unique among agencies that support scientific research. It was born of special circumstances that will probably never be duplicated. The transformation of the PRF from a pre-World War II oil company into a trust fund that continues to finance a wide range of basic research is a story likely to remain unparalleled.

The Petroleum Research Fund was created in 1944 when the owners of Universal Oil Products Company (UOP or Universal) donated the company's capital assets to the fund. The owners were seven major oil companies: Phillips Petroleum Company, Shell Oil Company, Standard Oil Company of California, Standard Oil Company (Indiana), Standard Oil Company (New Jersey), the Texas Company, and N. V. de Bataafsche Petroleum Maatschappij. UOP had developed the process of thermal cracking, known as the Dubbs process, which used extreme heat and pressure to break up hydrocarbons to produce gasoline. The seven oil companies had acquired Universal in 1931 and made a great deal of money licensing Universal's patents. The owners took advantage of their joint ownership by engaging in a system of sharing patents known as "cross-licensing," a practice that raised serious questions of compliance with antitrust laws. By the early 1940s the company faced formidable legal challenges. However, the federal government let Universal continue operating during World War II because the Allied military needed the company's technology to produce high-octane gasoline and aviation fuel. As the end of the war approached, in the summer of 1944 it was clear that the antitrust investigations would resume. The owners of Universal were unwilling to face the negative publicity that would result from defending their actions. Also in 1944, the United States Supreme Court handed down a verdict against UOP in a patent infringement case. Finally, the company was indirectly implicated in a scandal that included allegations about bribing a federal judge.

Universal's seven corporate owners wanted to dispose of UOP, but because of its legal problems buyers were unlikely. It was decided to donate UOP for charitable purposes, and in September 1944 the American Chemical Society was approached with a donation offer. Because outright ownership of the company by ACS was not feasible, a trust entitled "The Petroleum Research Fund," consisting of the capital stock of Universal, was drafted. Guaranty Trust Company of New York was named the trustee and ACS was named as qualified recipient of the income. The trust agreement stated that income from the trust was to be used to support "advanced scientific education and fundamental research in the petroleum field." The trust document further stated that the petroleum field could include "any area of pure science that could form the basis of subsequent research directly connected with the petroleum field." As the income recipient, ACS had the sole responsibility of determining what topics would fulfill those criteria. All parties signed the agreement on October 26, 1944, just fifty days after the initial approach to ACS.

The trust did not immediately bear fruit, however, since Universal was still in financial difficulty. David W. Harris, an electrical engineer with a talent for management, was hired as president of UOP. He settled lawsuits on the best possible terms, using the most recent technology from Universal's laboratories as negotiating tools. The most important technical achievement of the Harris era was the development and licensing of "Platforming," the reforming of petroleum in the presence of a platinum-containing catalyst. Development of the "Platforming" catalysts stands as one of the major advances in the petroleum industry of that era and was spearheaded by Vladimir Haensel, a young engineer whose technical achievements complemented Harris's managerial accomplishments.

By 1954 enough income had accumulated in the PRF Trust for the ACS Board of Directors to authorize the first grant programs supported by the funds. About $164,000 was awarded that year and by 1960 the amount was greater than $2.75 million. At the end of 1955 the trustee decided to sell the UOP securities, a move that would permit Universal to use its income for its own business purposes and provide the trust with the diversified portfolio required to support an ongoing grants program. The plan met strong legal opposition from small refiners who feared that the new owners would not share new technologies developed by Universal. Terms were worked out to meet all of the objections.

Since 1954, more than 13,000 grants valued at over $310 million have been awarded.

The stock in Universal was sold publicly but the amount of stock each buyer could purchase was limited so that no single person or company could own the technologies outright. The final court orders were filed in 1960 and approximately $70 million was realized from the sale. In the forty years of its existence as a diversified portfolio, the value of the PRF Trust has grown from $70 million to over $550 million at the end of 1999. In 1999 ACS distributed about $17 million in grants. Since 1954, more than thirteen thousand grants valued at over $310 million have been awarded.

PRF support of research at undergraduate institutions

Part of the charge to PRF contained in the trust agreement is to support "advanced scientific education." This requirement is taken very seriously by ACS-PRF staff and the Petroleum Research Fund Advisory Board. (It is the advisory board that makes the final recommendations on which projects to support.) Favoring proposals in which students at some level (undergraduate, graduate, or postdoctoral) are involved significantly in each research project fulfills that function. Usually, those students are supported by stipends paid by the grant.

Since its beginning, the Petroleum Research Fund has considered support of research at undergraduate institutions to be of special significance. When the first ACS-PRF advisory committee began looking at ways to use the PRF income, the importance of having undergraduate students involved in research was recognized. Since today's undergraduates become tomorrow's graduate students, faculty members and industrial researchers, providing research opportunities early in their scientific careers was considered extremely beneficial.

When the first ACS-PRF advisory committee began looking at ways to use the PRF income, the importance of having undergraduate students involved in research was recognized.

During the first few years of PRF's grant making, six different programs developed. Perhaps preferring simplicity to creativity, these programs were given the labels A, B, C, D, E, and F. Over the next fifteen years, some of the programs were dropped, two were combined, and a program of starter grants for new faculty was initiated. These starter grants are for faculty who are in the first three years of a regular faculty appointment and who do not have extensive postdoctoral research experience. Not wishing to break tradition, the new grant program was called Type G. Thus, the three research grant programs active today are denoted as Type AC, Type B, and Type G (page 178). Interestingly, the one program of the original six that remains is the Type B program that is

175

intended to support research involving undergraduate students in departments that do not offer the doctoral degree. In addition, applications to the Type G program are subdivided based upon the highest degree granted in the applicant's department. Type G applications from faculty holding positions in non-Ph.D.-granting departments are given the designation Type GB and are considered in competition only with applications from new faculty in similar departments. The Type AC program is open to faculty at undergraduate institutions, but the vast majority of AC grants are awarded to faculty in doctoral departments. In addition, a small Summer Research Fellowship (SRF) program allows holders of active PRF grants to apply for a supplement in order to provide support so that a faculty member from a non-doctoral department may participate in the PRF-funded research project.

Since the 1950s, more than three thousand Type B or GB grants have been awarded to faculty in undergraduate institutions. Thousands of undergraduate students have benefited from PRF research grants. Each year approximately 15 to 20 percent of the PRF grant budget supports these programs. Usually, about 30 to 40 percent of the Type B and GB applications are selected for grants. Even though these success rates are fairly good, that means that about two thirds of the applicants are denied. Thus, persistence and refining one's research ideas by considering the comments of reviewers is important for long term success.

PRF criteria and special features

PRF grants are an important source of funding for faculty in undergraduate institutions but may not be appropriate to support all research projects. PRF staff encourage applicants to talk with a program officer early in the proposal process. It is important that applicants understand the goals and mission of PRF, or whatever agency to which they intend to apply, before making the considerable effort to prepare a research proposal. To be accepted, all projects must first meet the guidelines stated in the PRF Trust Agreement:

It is important that applicants understand the goals and mission of PRF.

> The recipient (ACS) shall use all funds exclusively for advanced scientific education and fundamental research in the "petroleum field," which may include any field of pure science which in the judgment of (ACS) may afford a basis for subsequent research directly connected with the petroleum field.

Note that fundamental research is required as opposed to applied research or methods development. The proposed research need not be directly connected to petroleum, but rather may provide a basis for subsequent research directly connected with the petroleum field.

Once the requirement noted above is fulfilled, the PRF Advisory Board makes relative rankings of proposals, and recommendations for funding, on the basis of the following criteria:

- The overall quality, significance, and scientific merit of the proposed research, including the extent to which it will increase basic knowledge or stimulate additional research.
- The extent to which advanced scientific education will be enhanced through the involvement of students in the research.
- The qualifications or potential of the principal investigator(s) and adequacy of the facilities to conduct the research.
- The extent to which the proposed research represents a new or independent area of investigation for the principal investigator(s).
- The impact of PRF funding the research, including the effect on the principal investigator's overall research program and financial needs. For example, established scientists are not encouraged to seek additional support from PRF for research that has substantial current funding.

The advisory board distributes the available funds based on the relative ranking of proposals. The ACS Board of Directors through its Committee on Grants and Awards makes the final approval of grants.

Several features distinguish the PRF grants program from federal programs. Because of the wording of the original trust agreement, the fund must support "fundamental research" as opposed to applied research. Many government programs now wish to see immediate applications. Because of the origin of the PRF relating to possibly illegal licensing of patents, the trust agreement contains a provision that states that "Every patent, United States or foreign, that shall be taken out by or on behalf of the recipient or by or on behalf of any individual or institution acting at the direction of or on

The fund must support "fundamental" research as opposed to applied research.

behalf of the recipient, shall be immediately dedicated to the public, royalty free." Hence, direct commercialization of work supported by PRF

177

PRF GRANT PROGRAMS

• **Type AC Grants**, the largest of the PRF grant programs, usually fund proposals from graduate departments, but undergraduate faculty may apply. Beginning in 1998, the maximum amount awarded is $90,000 over three years. Most AC grants will provide $60,000 over two years. The budget submitted may include stipends for graduate students, undergraduates, or postdoctoral fellows, summer faculty salary, research supplies, travel costs, and a $500 annual departmental allocation.

• **Type B Grants** are restricted to departments which do not award the Ph.D. The fundamental research proposed must include participation by undergraduate students. Graduate students may not be supported with Type B funds. Budget may include undergraduate student stipends, summer faculty salary, supplies and equipment, travel costs, and a $500 annual departmental allocation. The average grant amount in 2000 was $12,335.

• **Type G "Starter" Grants** are intended for new faculty at U.S. institutions within the first three years of a regular appointment and without "extensive" postdoctoral research experience. The award amount is $25,000 over two years and a detailed budget is not required. A Type G grant may fund student stipends, summer faculty salary, supplies and equipment, and travel. Upon receipt by the PRF, Type G applications are subdivided based upon the highest degree granted in the applicant's department. Type G applications from faculty holding positions in non-Ph.D.-granting departments are considered in competition only with applications from faculty in similar departments.

• **Summer Research Fellowships** are awarded as supplements to active ACS-PRF grants. These fellowships are intended to support faculty guest researchers from non-doctoral institutions. A fellowship for $6,500 is provided to support a faculty visitor.

• **Scientific Education Grants** support a variety of projects designed to enhance ". . . advanced scientific education and fundamental research in the 'petroleum field'. . ." may be considered. Most awards provide partial funding for foreign speakers at major symposia in the United States or Canada.[1]

does not occur. PRF grants do not allow overhead or indirect costs to be charged, so that all of the funds awarded are available to support the research projects.

Although the size of individual PRF grants is small compared to federal grants, the impact of the grants is significant. Many faculty researchers have used PRF grants to jump-start their careers or to provide seed money for taking their research programs in new directions. For example, Henry Taube, winner of the 1983 Nobel Prize in chemistry, has credited the PRF with helping set up his research lab. It enabled him to pursue the work on electron transfer reactions that eventually led to the Nobel Prize. Another Nobel laureate, John Pople, received a PRF grant about ten years before receiving his Nobel Prize. Pople used computational models to study chemical structures, how molecules interact, and determine reaction pathways. The experience gained through this PRF-supported project has been useful in extending Dr. Pople's studies to many significant and diverse problems.

As noted earlier, thousands of undergraduate and graduate students, as well as postdoctoral fellows, have benefited from PRF grants, not just Nobel Prize winners. Many faculty credit the PRF with having a major impact on their early careers. However, mid-career and emeritus faculty also receive funding from PRF and the scientific education of their students is certainly enhanced by exposure to these research projects. More than fifty years after the formation of the Petroleum Research Fund it is impossible to know what its donors envisioned the outcome would be. However, we can be sure that they would be pleased with the extremely positive impact their contribution has made to the scientific research enterprise. Æ

FACULTY AND ADMINISTRATORS NEED to be keenly aware that support for scientific research is based on the interplay of factors beyond the strength of the proposed science. At a primarily undergraduate institution, the motivation to scholarship and the environment in which that scholarship is pursued are the keys—crucial keys—necessary for the development of career-long teachers-mentors-researchers. These faculty advance science, enhance institutional excellence, and provide the research-rich programs that our undergraduate students need and want.

Raymond Kellman is Senior Associate at Research Corporation.

Raymond Kellman

13 THE KEYS TO THE KINGDOM: MOTIVATION AND ENVIRONMENT

My objective here is to present those factors that are, in my belief and based on my own experiences as one of Research Corporation's agents in the field, crucial to the development and maintenance of strong individual research programs by faculty at primarily undergraduate institutions. The characteristics of such model programs include consistent, enthusiastic and meaningful undergraduate involvement, consistent outside funding and consistent production of peer-reviewed publications. Prolific publication is an unreasonable expectation for this setting.

This model is ideal, to be sure, and there are others that we applaud, highly value and readily fund. Nevertheless, it is this ideal that we look for and encourage chemists and physicists at undergraduate institutions to aspire to. In my interactions with our clientele, while I don't find this ideal program in abundance, I do find it regularly but not often enough.

To be successful a faculty member needs to have been blessed with the "right stuff." That "stuff" includes personal motivation and the ability to generate independent research ideas of significance—scientifically important ideas which are intellectually one's own. Significant scientific ideas are a *sine qua non* for doing research. Clearly, some scientists are a font of novel ideas while others struggle to find even one. For those who struggle, developing an independent research program is neither likely nor advisable. There are avenues in academe other than research that offer opportunities for significant and satisfying contributions to science and science education.

Some scientists are a font of novel ideas while others struggle to find even one.

In the undergraduate setting, chemists and physicists who have significant and fundable research ideas are plentiful, but strong research programs are not nearly so common. Why? Having encountered faculty of all stripes and colors and in every academic setting imaginable, from the hellish to the celestial, the overriding factors for success in research are individual motivation and institutional environment. There are a host of reasons that propel faculty to pursue scientific research in the undergraduate environment, a setting that is different from and in many ways more difficult than that in which our colleagues at Research I institutions labor. It is the nature of one's motivation that holds the key for success in research over time. Though both are vital, strong individual motivation can trump a poor institutional environment virtually every time.

Motivation

Though research-active faculty—a fraction of whom are research-productive—are motivated by all kinds of things, in virtually every instance, these can be reduced to a few core reasons. Granted, there are differences of degree and considerable complexity here, and we clearly recognize that faculty scientists have more than one prime motivation. Yet, in the end, one can usually point to a dominant single driving force.

All too common and obvious among faculty is the motivation to do research in order to secure tenure. This is, of course, the survival instinct at work, appropriate to life in the wilderness but a poor long-term motivation in an academic setting. The research program for these faculty typically dissipates shortly after a positive tenure decision; research is a burden rather than an exciting challenge. There are implications about the environment in such cases. Clearly, it suggests poor hiring practices and may signal problems within the department and institution. In the

All too common among faculty is the motivation to do research in order to secure tenure.

worst case, the positive tenure decision will often occur with residual resentment on both sides. The newly tenured faculty member resents both having had to do what he or she would rather not have done *and* probably having not done it very well—a self esteem problem. At least some departmental colleagues will be displeased that the person in question was not what they thought they hired six years earlier. This situation obviously degrades morale and the research environment.

Less common but more preferable in such cases is the early disappearance of any research program as well as the faculty member before the end of the six-year probationary period. This outcome, while not a happy one, is better for all. Such an outcome also sends a strong signal about the research environment, and a department's and institution's ability to make tough decisions. (Incidentally, a serious third-year review of faculty on six-year probationary appointments goes a long way toward ameliorating this problem.)

More successful but still problematic are faculty whose research is motivated by what one can term the "martyr complex." These self-sacrificing faculty are motivated to do research for the good of the students and their college or institution. These are faculty who never turn a student away or decline a request for service work. This is, without question, motivation that is noble, altruistic, and good. But it is self-sacrificial and ultimately destructive of scholarship. It may carry a faculty member's independent research program well beyond the probationary period, but rarely does it sustain a productive research program for the better part of a person's career.

These faculty just don't get that key proposal or manuscript submitted when it is crucial for sustaining their independent research programs. When, over the long haul, the going gets tough—with outside funding or institutional problems for example—too many faculty of this ilk slide into a program of student "research experiences" and away from productive, publishable research. The outcome of their endeavors changes from peer-reviewed publications with undergraduate coauthors and major presentations at national meetings to internal reports or theses that rarely see the light of day, and presentations in exclusively undergraduate venues. These activities may be good and have local value but they are not characteristic of excellence in research. These scientists may consider themselves research-active, but they are not research-productive. This group is most abundant and most influenced by institutional environment. Consequently, faculty so motivated are vulnerable and their research programs risk collapse.

As a foundation representative, dealing with self-sacrificing faculty members is very frustrating because they are but one step away, perhaps too large a step, from the motivational drive that I believe can sustain a productive undergraduate research program over an academic lifetime. *That* motivation is self-centered—intellectually self-centered. This is more noble and ultimately more altruistic than the self-sacrificing approach. These faculty are driven by their innate intellectual curiosity, the need to explore and discover. To use a well-worn phase, they display a "fire in the belly." They have to do research for themselves.

As teachers, mentors and researchers, they are complete scholars, and there are far too few of them at colleges and research universities.

How then do they differ from our colleagues who toil at Research I universities? The answer is "not at all." The PUI (primarily undergraduate institution) faculty member so motivated, simply must explore and share the excitement of discovery with students. To do that, he or she recognizes that teaching and mentoring are crucial, part and parcel, to their overall scholarly endeavors and are equally committed to them. They are teachers, mentors and researchers. In short, they are complete scholars, and there are far too few of them at the colleges *and* at the research universities. In the undergraduate setting these individuals write the proposals, do the science and submit manuscripts to share their findings because they need to. When they do, outside funding, good students and professional recognition accrue to this scholar, to their students and the institution. These faculty have coattails. They generate an excitement and enthusiasm that energizes students and colleagues alike. To them institutional problems generally seem smaller and more soluble. If not, then these faculty members, who are "self-centered" rather than "self-sacrificing" may conclude that they have outgrown the institution and can comfortably and confidently move on to an academic environment better suited to their scholarly aspirations. The venue may change but their contributions to the advancement of science will continue. For these scientists individual motivation trumps environment.

Environment

What about the institutional environment? There are no secrets here. A strong positive environment is for the faculty the tide that raises all boats. A negative environment is an ebb and has a faculty scientist struggling through the mire and muck. Individuals operating in a positive environment will usually exceed the expectations of their peers and of themselves. They thrive and grow intellectually, scientifically and personally. When placed in a negative setting few excel; those who do are always the "self-centered," but none remain unscathed by the experience.

The advancement of science through research is Research Corporation's mission. We achieve that by investing in individual careers and in institutions. We know our clientele and the environments in which they do scholarly research. To invest wisely, we *need* to know. Institutional visits are a hallmark of Research Corporation. When making a campus visit as a Research Corporation representative, nothing is easier to gauge or read than the prevailing academic environment.

Nothing is easier to gauge than the prevailing academic environment, and nothing is more difficult to change.

Given the difficulties that the teacher-mentor-researcher must overcome to establish and maintain a productive research program at a PUI, institutional environment is an important consideration in making individual awards through our Cottrell College Science Award (CCSA) program. For our Department Development program, a collective award made to foster a tide that raises all boats in a chemistry or physics department or both, institutional environment is paramount. Though hardly the complete story, it is telling that over the last five or six years Research Corporation has made more than four hundred individual CCS awards but only four Department Development awards.

The composite elements of a strong environment are resources and facilities, communication, mutual understanding and respect, leadership, camaraderie, and, of course, history. Institutional history is an amazing thing. I am convinced that a "genetic component" is at work. In an over-whelming number of cases departmental and institutional strengths and weaknesses of the past are replicated in each new generation. Players change but the problems of the fifties, became the problems of the seventies and are now the problems of the early twenty-first century. Administrative indiffer-ence to science, departments beset with infighting, poor facilities and facilities support—all problems which debilitate scientific research and scholarship—become "genetically" characteristic of an institution. Can this cycle ever be broken, and if so, how? Energetic and visionary leader-ship can and does transform science departments and institutions. Un-fortunately, this is uncommon, but when it does occur a science depart-ment has a singular and fleeting opportunity to break out and move to a new level of excellence, to make an evolutionary change. Research Cor-poration is always looking for these opportunities.

Departmental strengths and weaknesses of the past are replicated in each new generation.

Tangible environmental elements, resources and facilities, are easiest to evaluate. They are also the easiest for an institution to change. Is adequate research space and the necessary modern instrumentation avail-able to a principal investigator? Are these maintained by the institution? Start-up packages need to be realistic and reasonable, and institutional financial support must to be ongoing. A start-up package of $50,000–100,000 demonstrates an excellent initial commitment, but will new money for matching be available? Will the unexpected or emergency faculty research need for $10,000 in future years be readily met? Are teaching loads reasonable, and do they factor in and value the teaching-mentoring efforts of the productive researcher? Can the research being proposed to Research Corporation be done in this undergraduate set-ting? With unsatisfactory answers to these questions, a high-quality CCSA proposal to undertake a significant and exciting research project may be deemed unfeasible in a given environment and would not be funded. (Department Development consideration is out of the question.)

More important and more elusive in an academic environment are the intangibles, mutual respect and understanding amongst colleagues within a department, between departments and vertically with administrators. These institutional virtues take serious effort to cultivate and maintain. Neglect them and they will certainly evaporate. If cultivated, trust and camaraderie seem to follow. For this to happen, good communication and good will are crucial. Strong academic leaders, from department chairs through presidents or chancellors, know this and work at it.

Until given reason to believe otherwise, one ought to assume good will exists among men and women in academe and, happily, this is overwhelmingly true. But alas, good communication is not the norm—and there's the rub. Good communication, particularly between scientists and their nonscientist colleagues who happen to make up the large fraction of college and university administrators, is not and has not been a strength. The problems that develop from a failure to communicate are, on some campuses, legendary. Respect and understanding are replaced by mistrust and ill will. In mild cases it distracts and annoys; in its more odious forms it demoralizes faculty, paralyzes scholarship and is significantly disadvantageous to students.

Rest assured that students quickly recognize a dysfunctional department and they resent it. How can this be dealt with? Never easily. It often begins with a third party, a foundation representative or consultants perceived as neutral, who can identify the problems and offer solutions. The diagnosis is usually straightforward and the cure of long duration.

The good news is that strong positive research environment in one segment of an academic community can be just as infectious as its pathogenic counterpart. We do find in some institutions Henry V's "band of brothers," within a chemistry or physics department. A research-active and productive department with this kind of camaraderie or esprit de corps can reach new heights of excellence in research, if provided with financial and advisory support. When appropriate, Research Corporation can provide such support. Often, but certainly not always, when one so stimulates to greater achievement a physics department, for example, the les-

> *A department with this esprit de corps can reach new heights of excellence in research.*

> ### RESEARCH CORPORATION FUNDING CRITERIA OF THE 1970S
>
> If . . . the primary reason for Research Corporation's interest in liberal arts colleges is the development not of more Ph.D.s, but of individuals likely to be better research workers than have been produced in the past, the odds must be examined more carefully in the future. It would seem wise . . . to concentrate more on the colleges of reasonably high selectivity—the "very selective" and higher. . . . Next, look for the good track record in terms of past productivities by the department. But, within the group of colleges which meet these criteria, yet other factors must be determined. They are the personal traits and the mental quality of the senior faculty members. The first three bits of information are available. The latter factors can best be evaluated by the Regional Representatives. Once such departments are identified, it might be wise to back them over longer periods of time.
>
> —*Twenty Five Years in Support of the Advancement of Science,*
> Research Corporation, 1970[1]

son is not lost, and increased scholarship will begin to show itself in other science departments, and perhaps even beyond.

Conclusion

At Research Corporation the decision to invest in individual scientists through our CCSA program is made by evaluating the science, the scientists and their environment. To advance science we believe that we need to invest in career development as much as in a specific research project. Except for those individuals at the extremes, these decisions are not easy. What about strong science from a driven chemist or physicist in weak or unsupportive institution? I believe in these cases the record shows that Research Corporation has overwhelmingly made positive decisions to provide support, that we come down on the side of the motivated scientist.

To advance science we need to invest in career development as much as in a specific research project.

But evaluating institutional environment is easier and can be done more quickly than assessing what drives a scientist. Motivation while perhaps more important is also more difficult to measure. Yet, the large majority of our clientele are beginning faculty, with no independent track record, and about whom we may know little. Surely, a publication record during one's apprenticeship in a

187

doctoral program and as a postdoctoral associate is a guide, but no more than that, and academic pedigree does not reliably predict future performance. Neither measures motivation with any certainty. Thus, more often than not we are left to decide on research proposed by faculty about whom we would wish to know more. Institutional environment naturally looms larger and weighs more heavily in any decision to make an award. The wealth generated in this nation during the nineties has left institutions including the PUIs with the resources to make very significant improvements to the environments in which their faculty teach and do research. This fact is not lost on us and raises institutional responsibility.

Faculty and administrators need to be keenly aware that support for scientific research is based on the interplay of factors beyond the strength of the proposed science. At a PUI, the motivation to scholarship and the environment in which that scholarship is pursued, are the keys—crucial keys—necessary for the development of career long teacher-mentors-researchers. These faculty advance science, enhance institutional excellence, and provide the research-rich programs that our undergraduate students need and want. It is in these careers that Research Corporation looks to invest. Æ

APPENDIX
SOME PROGRAMS FOR UNDERGRADUATE INSTITUTIONS

THE CAMILLE AND HENRY DREYFUS FOUNDATION

START-UP GRANTS FOR UNDERGRADUATE INSTITUTIONS

The Camille and Henry Dreyfus Faculty Start-up Grant Program was introduced in 1993 to provide funding for new faculty members at non-Ph.D.-granting institutions at the start of their research and teaching activities. While most talented young faculty are able to secure external research support, in most cases such support does not ordinarily become available before the end of the first year of appointment. Thus, a key feature of the award is an unrestricted research grant that is awarded in September of the year the new faculty member formally begins the first-year appointment. In general, ten awards are made each year based on institutional nominations.

Eligibility: Only faculty members who start their first full-time tenure-track appointments between January 1 and December 31 in the year of the award are eligible. Institutions that grant a bachelor's or master's degree, but not a doctorate, in chemistry, chemical engineering or biochemistry may submit nominations. Nominees are normally expected to have no more than three years of postdoctoral experience.

The complete guidelines can be found on the foundation's Web site, www.dreyfus.org.

THE SCHOLAR/FELLOW PROGRAM

The Camille and Henry Dreyfus Scholar/Fellow Program for Undergraduate Institutions is designed to attract talented Ph.D. recipients to careers in the chemical sciences in undergraduate colleges and universities, and to recognize outstanding research by faculty from predominantly undergraduate institutions. The dual-purpose program provides a grant to the institution on behalf of an established faculty member, designated the Camille and Henry Dreyfus Scholar. The award is intended to enhance and enrich the Scholar's research and teaching. It is also designed to provide the Fellow with an understanding of the traditional operations of an undergraduate department and with an appreciation of the commitment by students and faculty to quality instruction.

Eligibility and Scope: The grant is to be used in part by the Scholar to appoint a recent Ph.D. recipient as a Camille and Henry Dreyfus Fellow. The Fellow will collaborate in research with the Scholar and teach in the department. The program is open to all departments of chemistry, chemical engineering and bio-chemistry in public and private institutions that do not award Ph.D. degrees in these fields. Faculty proposed as Scholars must hold a full-time tenure-track positions for a total of at least ten years, with at least five years at the current institution.

The Fellow is expected to have a teaching assignment that is meaningful but still allows significant research collaboration with the Scholar. The remainder of the award is to be used by the Camille and Henry Dreyfus Scholar for research or educational purposes.

The complete guidelines and online application can be found on the foundation's Web site, www.dreyfus.org.

CAMILLE DREYFUS TEACHER-SCHOLAR AWARD
HENRY DREYFUS TEACHER-SCHOLAR AWARD

In 1969, the Camille and Henry Dreyfus Foundation established the Camille and Henry Dreyfus Teacher-Scholar Awards Program to strengthen the teaching and research careers of talented young faculty in the chemical sciences. Based on institutional nominations, the program was designed to provide discretionary funding to faculty at early stages in their careers. Criteria for selection included a commitment to education and an independent body of scholarship that signaled the promise of continuing outstanding contributions to both research and teaching.

Both programs are intended to encourage young scholars who embrace and amalgamate the academic research and teaching missions. However, the two programs have different emphases. The Camille Dreyfus Teacher-Scholar Awards Program is focused primarily on individual research attainment and promise, but evidence of excellence in teaching is also expected. The Henry Dreyfus Teacher-Scholar Awards Program stresses teaching, mentorship, and the nominees' accomplishments in research and teaching primarily with undergraduates.

Eligibility: Institutions may submit only one Camille Dreyfus or one Henry Dreyfus nomination annually. Institutions that grant a bachelor's or higher degree in chemistry, chemical engineering, or biochemistry may submit nominations to the Henry Dreyfus Teacher-Scholar Awards Program. Nominees must hold a full-time tenure-track academic appointment, be between the fourth and ninth years of their independent academic careers and engage in teaching and research primarily with undergraduates.

The complete guidelines can be found on the foundation's Web site, www.dreyfus.org.

RESEARCH CORPORATION

COTTRELL COLLEGE SCIENCE AWARDS

The Cottrell College Science Awards are designed to provide summer support for research in astronomy, chemistry and physics at public and private, predominantly undergraduate institutions in the United States and Canada. The projects proposed are judged on the basis of originality, significance and feasibility; also taken into account is the potential of the research for involving undergraduate students in a collegial relationship. After review by the foundation staff and outside referees, proposals are evaluated by an advisory committee drawn from the academic science community. Awards are made to the institution on behalf of the individual investigator(s) following approval by the foundation's board of directors.

Eligibility: The principal investigator must have an appointment in a department of astronomy, chemistry or physics, which offers at least baccalaureate, but not doctoral, degrees.

Criteria: The potential of a proposed research project to add to fundamental scientific knowledge is the prime criterion in its evaluation. Other factors are college research support, student participation, and the contribution the research will make to the college's science programs.

Funding: Cottrell College Science Awards, approved for one or two years, provide direct expenses necessary to the proposed research:

- Equipment and supplies
- Student summer stipends
- Faculty summer stipends
- Services or requirements essential to the research

The complete program guidelines and application request forms can be found on the foundation's Web site, www.rescorp.org.

Cottrell College Science Awards, Funding Rates 1989–1999

Year	89	90	91	92	93	94	95	96	97	98	99
Total Proposals	262	193	226	187	221	228	243	250	241	244	236
Total Awards	143	94	92	77	100	94	97	82	74	73	74

NATIONAL SCIENCE FOUNDATION

COURSE, CURRICULUM AND LABORATORY IMPROVEMENT PROGRAM

The CCLI program seeks to improve the quality of science, mathematics, engineering, and technology (SMET) education for all students and targets activities affecting learning environments, course content, curricula, and educational practices. The program has three tracks:

Educational Materials Development (CCLI-EMD) projects are expected to produce innovative materials that incorporate effective educational practices to improve student learning of SMET. Two types of EMD projects are supported: (a) those that intend to demonstrate the scientific and educational feasibility of an idea, a "proof of concept" or prototype, and (b) those based on prior experience with a prototype that intend to fully develop the product or practice.

Adaptation and Implementation (CCLI-A&I) projects are expected to result in improved education in SMET at academic institutions through adaptation and implementation of exemplary materials, laboratory experiences, and/or educational practices that have been developed and tested at other institutions. Proposals may request funds in any category normally supported by NSF, or may request funds to purchase only instrumentation.

National Dissemination (CCLI-ND) projects are expected to provide faculty with professional development opportunities to enable them to introduce new content into undergraduate courses and laboratories, and to explore effective educational practices to improve their teaching effectiveness. Projects should be designed to offer workshops, short courses, or similar activities on a national scale in single or multiple disciplines.

Eligibility: Proposals are invited from organizations in the U. S. and its territories: two-year colleges, four-year colleges, universities, professional societies, consortia of institutions, nonprofit and for-profit organizations.

In 1999 the CCLI programs received a total of 1056 proposals and funded 316; 351 of 1041 proposals were funded in 2000. Complete guidelines and application procedures can be found on the NSF Web site, www.ehr.nsf.gov/EHR/DUE/programs/ccli.

RESEARCH EXPERIENCES FOR UNDERGRADUATES PROGRAM

The REU Program, modeled in part on the earlier and successful Undergraduate Research Participation (URP) Program, was initiated in 1986 as one means of attracting talented students into scientific research careers. The REU program seeks to provide educational experiences for undergraduate students through research participation. REU projects involve students in ongoing research projects specially designed for the purpose. The projects feature high-quality interaction of students with faculty and other research mentors and access to facilities and professional development opportunities.

REU "Sites" are established in all fields of science, mathematics, and engineering for a period of one to five years. Each Site consists of a group of ten or so undergraduates who work in the research programs of the host institution. Students are accepted from throughout the country. Each student is assigned to a specific research project, and works closely with faculty, postdocs, and graduate students for eight to ten weeks during the summer. In addition, seminars, lunch meetings, and social functions are organized to facilitate interaction between the undergraduates. Students are granted stipends, and in some cases assistance with housing and travel.

More information can be found at www.nsf.gov/home/crssprgm/reu/start.htm.

RESEARCH IN UNDERGRADUATE INSTITUTIONS PROGRAM

The specific objectives of the RUI Program are to support high-quality research by faculty with active involvement of undergraduate students; to strengthen the research environment in academic departments that are oriented primarily toward undergraduate instruction; and to promote the integration of research and education.

Eligibility: While the involvement of undergraduates is an important feature of RUI, the overriding purpose is the support of faculty research. Proposals may be submitted by individual faculty or groups of collaborating investigators and are accepted in all fields of science and engineering supported by the NSF including research on learning and education.

Funding: Proposals for RUI faculty research projects may request support for salaries and wages, research assistantships, fringe benefits, travel, materials and supplies, publication costs and page charges, consultant services, essential equipment, field work, research at other institutions, and indirect costs. The RUI also provides support for shared-use instrumentation or other research tools.

More information can be found at www.ehr.nsf.gov/crssprgm/rui/program.shtm.

RUI Research Awards in the Physical Sciences, Funding Rates 1989–1999*

Year	89	90	91	92	93	94	95	96	97	98	99
Total Proposals	109	130	107	125	114	122	123	117	132	107	127
Total Awards	43	53	46	61	41	58	42	46	61	32	32

*Divisions of Astronomical Sciences, Chemistry, Materials Research, and Physics.

REFERENCES AND FURTHER READING

CHAPTER 1

1. W. A. Patrick, "What Kind of Research is Essential to Good Teaching?" *Journal of Chemical Education* 1 (1924): 16

2. H. N. Holmes, "College Research," *Journal of Chemical Education* 1 (1924): 81

3. James C. Baughman and Robert N. Goldman, "College Rankings and Faculty Publications: Are They Related?" *Change* 31, no. 2 (1999): 44–50.

4. Ernest L. Boyer, *College: The Undergraduate Experience in America* (New York: Harper and Row, 1987).

5. Ernest L. Boyer, *Scholarship Reconsidered: Priorities of the Professoriate* (Princeton: The Carnegie Foundation for the Advancement of Teaching, 1990).

6. Ibid., 83–126.

7. James C. Baughman and Robert N. Goldman, "College Rankings and Faculty Publications: Are They Related?" *Change* 31, no. 2 (1999): 44–50.

8. *College*, 131.

9. *Scholarship Reconsidered*, 81.

10. David Davis-Van Atta, Sam C. Carrier, and Frank Frankfort, "Educating America's Scientists: The Role of the Research Colleges," report of The Future of Science at Liberal Arts Colleges Conference (Oberlin College, 1985).

11. Ibid., 35.

12. Sam C. Carrier and David Davis-Van Atta, "Maintaining America's Scientific Productivity: The Necessity of the Liberal Arts Colleges," final report of The Future of Science at Liberal Arts Colleges Conference (Oberlin College, 1987): 2–3.

CHAPTER 2

1. Research Corporation, *Twenty Five Years in Support of the Advancement of Science: An Evaluation of the Grants Programs of Research Corporation, 1945–1970*, report (New York: Research Corporation, 1970).

2. Ernest L. Boyer, *Scholarship Reconsidered, Priorities of the Professoriate* (Princeton: The Carnegie Foundation for the Advancement of Teaching, 1990): 55.

3. James N. Spencer and Claude H. Yoder. "A Survey of Undergraduate Research Over the Past Decade," *Journal of Chemical Education* 58 (October 1981): 780.

CHAPTER 3

1. Sheila Tobias, *They're Not Dumb, They're Different: Stalking the Second Tier* (Tucson, Ariz.: Research Corporation, 1990): 9–10.

2. Leo Reisberg, "Research by Undergraduates Proliferates, but Is Some of It Just Glorified Homework?" *The Chronicle of Higher Education* 37 (May 22, 1998): A45.

CHAPTER 4

1. National Science Foundation, *Undergraduate Origins of Recent (1991– 1995) Science and Engineering Doctorate Recipients*, NSF 96-334 (Arlington, Va.: 1996).

2. T. C. Werner, Robert L. Lichter, and Thomas R. Krugh, "The National Conferences on Undergraduate Education (NCUR®): Conference History and the Role of Chemistry," *Journal of Chemical Education*, in press.

Suggested reading for "Time Management:"

Baldwin, B. A. *It's All in Your Head*. Wilmington, N.C.: Direction Dynamics, 1985.

Covey, S. R. *The 7 Habits of Highly Effective People: Powerful Lessons in Personal Change*. New York: Fireside, 1989.

Schlenger, Sunny, and Roberta Roesh. *How to be Organized in Spite of Yourself*. New York: Signet, 1990.

CHAPTER 5

1. National Academy of Sciences, *Opportunities in Chemistry* (Washington: National Academy Press, 1985).

2. C.P. Snow, *The Two Cultures and the Scientific Revolution* (Cambridge University Press: 1959).

3. Ernest L. Boyer, *Scholarship Reconsidered, Priorities of the Professoriate* (Princeton: The Carnegie Foundation for the Advancement of Teaching, 1990): 55.

4. Jerry R. Mohrig and Douglas C. Neckers, *Laboratory Experiments in Organic Chemistry* (New York: Van Nostrand, 1968).

5. For the text of Richard P. Feynman's 1961–1962 lectures in introductory physics at Caltech, see: Richard P. Feynman, Robert B. Leighton, and Matthew L. Sands, *The Feynman Lectures on Physics: Commemorative Issue* (Redwood City, Calif: Addison-Wesley, 1989).

CHAPTER 6

1. C. E. Glassick, M. Taylor Huber, G.I. Maeroff, *Scholarship Assessed: Evaluation of the Professoriate* (San Francisco: Jossey Bass, 1997).

2. Ibid., 36.

3. National Science Foundation, "Awards Cite Undergraduate College Plans to Integrate Research and Education," press release, September 23, 1998.

4. J. N. Spencer and C. H. Yoder, "The Past Two Decades of Undergraduate Research," *Journal of Chemical Education* 78 (1995): 146.

5. E. Garfield, "The Role of Undergraduate Colleges in Research. Part 2: Highest Impact Institutions and Most Cited Papers, 1981–1992." *Current Contents* 25 (1993): 3–9.

6. Project Kaleidoscope Web site, www.pkal.org

CHAPTER 7

1. Sheila Tobias, *Revitalizing Undergraduate Education: Why Some Things Work and Most Don't* (Tucson, Ariz: Research Corporation, 1993): 13.

2. Project Kaleidoscope, *What Works: Building Natural Sciences Communities,* occasional paper, 1991: 63.

3. Ibid., 88–89.

4. Ibid., 54.

5. Michael P. Doyle, "A Brief History of the Council on Undergraduate Research: The Early Years," CUR *Newsletter* (December 1991): 17–23.

CHAPTER 8

1. Division of Chemistry, National Science Foundation, "Report on the NSF Workshop on Research in the Undergraduate Curriculum," 1991: 2.

2. "Undergraduate Research and Departmental Fund-Raising," CUR *Quarterly* (March 1999).

3. For the most recent figures see: "ACS Committee on Professional Training 1996 Annual Report," *Chemical and Engineering News* (February 2, 1998): 35–42. Furman is listed with 25 ACS-certified bachelor's degrees, up from 10 in 1989.

4. ACS Committee on Professional Training, "Undergraduate Professional Education in Chemistry: Guidelines and Evaluation Procedures," (Washington: American Chemical Society, 1999): 11.

5. Survey of Earned Doctorates, sponsored by five Federal agencies [National Science Foundation, National Institutes of Health, National Endowment for the Humanities, U.S. Department of Education, and U.S. Department of Agriculture], and conducted by the National Research Council.

CHAPTER 9

1. NIH Web site, http://grants.nih.gov/grants/funding/area_appl_awds.htm

CHAPTER 11

1. Ernest L. Eliel, *Science and Serendipity: The importance of basic research* (Washington: American Chemical Society, 1992): 14.

CHAPTER 12

1. PRF Web site, www.acs.org/prf

Bibliography for Chapter 12

Frost, Pam. "The Petroleum Research Fund." *Chemistry* (Winter 1999): 12–14.

Collat, Justin W. "UOP and PRF: How The Petroleum Research Fund Came To Be." *Chemical Heritage* 12 (Summer 1995).

CHAPTER 13

1. Research Corporation, *Twenty Five Years in Support of the Advancement of Science: An Evaluation of the Grants Programs of Research Corporation, 1945–1970*, report (New York: Research Corporation, 1970): 26–27.

FURTHER READING

Council on Undergraduate Research. *Directory of Research in Chemistry at Primarily Undergraduate Institutions,* 7th edition. CUR, 1999. (Data from 1994–1996 only.)

—— *Research in Biology at Primarily Undergraduate Institutions.* Eds., Mary M. Allen and Laura L.M. Hoopes. Holland, Mich., 1989.

National Research Council. *Assessing the Value of Research in the Chemical Sciences.* Report of a workshop. Washington: National Academy Press, 1998.

—— *Research Teams and Partnerships: Trends in the Chemical Sciences.* Report of a workshop. Washington: National Academy Press, 1999.

—— *Graduate Education in the Chemical Science—Issues for the 21st Century.* Report of a workshop. Washington: National Academy Press, 2000.

—— *Laboratory Design, Construction and Renovation: Participants, process and product.* Washington: National Academy Press, 2000.

Project Kaleidoscope. *Faculty for the 21st Century, A Collection of Statements 1998–1999.*

Research Corporation. "The Midas Touch: Do Soaring Endowments Have Any Impact on College Science?" Annual report, 1998.

Snelling, W. Rodman, and Robert F. Boruch. *Science in Liberal Arts Colleges: A Longitudinal Study of 49 Selective Colleges.* New York: Columbia University Press, 1972.

ACADEMIC EXCELLENCE:

A Study of the Role of Research in the Natural Sciences at Undergraduate Institutions

Sponsored by:
The Camille and Henry Dreyfus Foundation
W. M. Keck Foundation
M. J. Murdock Charitable Trust
Research Corporation
The Robert A. Welch Foundation

FIVE FOUNDATIONS CONCERNED ABOUT the quality of science in predominantly undergraduate institutions have initiated a study of factors that sustain faculty and students in the natural sciences. Individually, the foundations are each aware of a multitude of changes that are taking place both in the education of students in science and in the professional development of faculty. Together, the foundations have agreed that a study of the environment that exists for the natural sciences at predominantly undergraduate institutions is timely.

The "Oberlin Reports" (see page 16) originated from two conferences that were designed to address an issue of particular importance to that time period: the disproportionately high production of students from predominantly undergraduate institutions who obtained their Ph.D. degrees in the sciences. Attended by the presidents of forty-eight liberal arts colleges in 1985 and of representatives from fifty such institutions in 1986, these conferences and reports set the stage for enhancement of science via numerous institutional and foundation developments during subsequent years. Given the concerns expressed about activities in science at predominantly undergraduate institutions today, a new study was judged to be necessary.

The core of the project is an examination of the environment for research in the natural sciences at undergraduate institutions. Involving in-depth reports from institutions invited to participate and analyses of these reports by capable scientists, the project will culminate in the publication of summary findings in June of 2001. Data obtained from participating institutions together with those available from government, foundations, and professional society sources are being compiled and analyzed to assess the environment for natural science and its operations at predominantly undergraduate institutions.

The study will provide previously unavailable information relevant to support for the natural sciences, the environment for research and the productivity of faculty at undergraduate institutions.